MY GOOD LIFE

V.W. Hilton

MINERVA PRESS
LONDON
ATLANTA MONTREUX SYDNEY

MY GOOD LIFE
Copyright © V.W. Hilton 1998

All Rights Reserved

No part of this book may be reproduced in any form
by photocopying or by any electronic or mechanical means,
including information storage or retrieval systems,
without permission in writing from both the copyright
owner and the publisher of this book.

ISBN 0 75410 446 X

First Published 1998 by
MINERVA PRESS
315–317 Regent Street
London W1R 7YB

Printed in Great Britain for Minerva Press

MY GOOD LIFE

To my wife Ella
for her patience and understanding

To my colleagues
of the City of Manchester
and the Greater Manchester Fire Service

Photographs are reproduced by permission of the Manchester Fire Service Museum

MY GOOD LIFE

To my wife Ella
for her patience and understanding

To my colleagues
of the City of Manchester
and the Greater Manchester Fire Service

Photographs are reproduced by permission of the Greater Manchester Fire Service Museum

What to Do

It all began the day I left the RAF after five years' service as a radio operator, three of those years spent abroad; let loose into civvy street again with four weeks' demob leave and a few bob in my pocket. Jobs were reasonably plentiful in those days, so I had time to look around. My first thoughts were to join the merchant navy as a radio officer, but having recently started to court the girl who was eventually to become my wife, it did not seem like a good idea to have to spend months away from home, so that idea got the boot.

A few days later, whilst walking through the town, I saw a group of firemen cleaning a fire engine outside the station; why not, I thought. So into station I went, to be confronted by a Scot built like Ben Nevis. I explained I was interested in joining the fire service, he promptly asked me what eight by eight was, I replied, 'Sixty four', and to this day I do not know what that had to do with my joining the fire service; but he took me into the office and gave me the application forms. I went off home and filled in the same and posted them to the County Fire Brigade HQ.

A couple of weeks elapsed and a letter arrived telling me to report to Eccles fire station on a Wednesday evening for aptitude tests and, if successful in those, a medical exam. Off I went on the appointed date where I met several other hopeful candidates; after half an hour or so of answering questions which did not appear to have anything to do with the fire service I was sent to be examined by a doctor.

Now at this time being a non-smoker and moderate drinker I considered myself to be as fit as the proverbial butcher's dog, and the doctor appeared to be satisfied with my health. Then the four of us who had been successful so far were taken down to the station yard and given a demonstration of a fireman's lift; we were paired off, and you had to carry your partner a specified distance in a specified time. After this exercise I was not so sure of my fitness as it certainly tested your stamina.

I went home to await a letter to see if I had been accepted or not. Three weeks later with money running out I received a letter to report to my local station at Ashton-under-Lyne on a Monday at 9 a.m. I arrived on the appointed date a lot earlier than I should have to be met by a fireman who took me to the canteen for a cuppa. I stood around till the oncoming watch reported for duty, then I was taken into the station office to be met by Ben Nevis who explained what was to be my routine for the day. First I was to be taken to Brigade HQ near Preston to be issued with all my equipment and to sign and have my contract explained to me.

On arrival at the HQ I was informed by a civilian that I was being accepted as a trainee fireman and that for the first two years of my service I was to be on probation. During this period of time I could be dismissed from the service at any time. Every six months the officer in charge gave a written assessment of your progress, which you read and then signed if you agreed with it. I was lucky enough not to find out what would have happened if I had disagreed with an assessment. My pay was to be around nine pounds a week before stoppages, but I well remember my first take-home pay was six pounds nineteen shillings (six pounds ninety-five). That was after stoppages for national insurance, income tax and superannuation contributions.

I was then taken to the stores where I was issued with all my fire gear plus ordinary uniform and three blankets and a kitbag. Back at the station I spent the rest of the day marking and cleaning all my newly issued gear which was in a rather messy state, and then sewing my brigade number on my fire tunics, mine was 251. At 5 p.m. we had a cup of tea in the canteen and the station officer told me I would be on day shift until I had been to training school; that meant 9 a.m. till 6 p.m. from Monday to Friday.

The following day when I reported for duty the lads showed me the routine of dressing into fire gear, being paraded and then detailed off for which appliance you would be on for that tour of duty. One man was detailed off to be on duty in the watchroom and another as mess orderly to assist the civvy cook and keep the mess room tidy. I was told to put my gear on the Pump/Escape and in the event of a fire I was to stick with the officer in charge. I could not wait for that first turn out, and throughout the tour I was on edge waiting and hoping for a shout; but I had no such luck for the first couple of days.

My third day on saw me go to my first cotton mill fire, this was before the complete demise of the Lancashire cotton industry. The fire was in the fanny hole, the area where the cotton bales were broken open prior to going onto a machine to be combed out. On arrival at the incident I was told to keep out of the way which I did, as the smoke to me appeared very thick, but I was eventually assured this was nothing. A couple of hours later we made up all the gear and put it back on the appliance, but the thing that left a big impression on me was that every man on the crew seemed to know his job without any shouting and bawling they just got on with it like a well-oiled machine.

Needless to say that when I got home in the evening what had been a minor fire became a major conflagration with its telling to my parents.

In the two weeks before I went to training school I got to know the guys on the station and the station routine; just listening to the conversations about the fires they had attended in the past fascinated me. Ashton fire station was virtually on one level, whilst there was a BA compressor in the basement and the locker room was above the dormitory the rest of the station was ground level. The front of the station looked out on the bus terminus and indoor market, the area in front of the engine house gates was huge so that the appliances never had a problem when we turned out.

The meals were cooked by an old lady who treated everyone the same with no favourites. The station officer and the sub officer sat at their own table, the rest of the lads sat together. We had a break at eleven o'clock followed by a full lunch at one o'clock, a cuppa at three thirty and at five we had a light tea such as beans on toast. For this we paid a weekly sum of ten bob (fifty pence), which was good value but nearby were the big indoor and outdoor markets and the traders were very good with our mess manager. For example on Saturday afternoons we got salads and the like from the traders, from goods that they had left over, and we quite often got cakes from the bakers' stalls. I myself would scrounge tripe and black puddings, these being one of my favourite foods and all these years later I still buy them when I get the chance, but I must say the black puddings are not as nice as they used to be. A good fatty pudding boiled and served with mustard and fresh bread takes a bit of beating.

It was during this period of waiting to go to the training school that I found out that the cleanliness of machines and equipment was next to godliness in the fire service, and at this time of my service the alloy standpipes and different equipment was still a way off. Brass was still the order of the day and this had to be polished till you could see your face in it, and there was still quite a bit of hose made of canvas about. I was to learn later that to darn a length of hose with hemp was a specialised job, the hose would be darned and the man doing it initialled it before it was tested up to a pressure of one hundred pounds per square inch and woe betide the man who had repaired it if it leaked badly from the darn.

Later the rubber lined hose was repaired in much the same way as a car inner tube, it was patched using a Stenorising machine, which welded a patch on the hose. The appliances themselves were kept in a high state of cleanliness, and highly polished bodywork. There were still a few old fire appliances about; the ones you stood on the side of en route to a fire, commonly known as Braidwoods, and which a few years later I had the honour of driving to fires. They were a challenge to drive with crash gearboxes and no power steering; they were packed with power but they needed driving.

Cleanliness of your fire gear was another important item. You were inspected in your fire gear every time you came on duty and excuses for dirty gear were not acceptable. The fire boots were made of leather and these had to be polished and your leggings had to be cleaned with boot polish; axe handles were scrubbed and the blade had to be bright so emery cloth was order of the day with that, and your belt and pouch were also polished with boot polish. It quickly became second nature to clean your gear before going off duty.

If your fire tunic was wet, that was put in the drying room and brushed off as soon as it was dry. We had three tunics issued to us but you always kept one for best, to be used for special parades. We were issued with four pairs of trousers, and again you always kept one pair nicely pressed and for use on special occasions.

The time soon came for me to pack my gear and go off to training school.

Training

The school was situated in an operational station at Morecambe. There were twenty-four of us for this course, and first we were shown our quarters, which were to be our home for the next six weeks. Then it was down to a lecture room to be addressed by the course commandant and our instructors.

Our instructor introduced himself thus 'My name is Sub O So and So and I am a bastard, sometimes a nice bastard but none the less an out and out bastard and don't you forget it.' It was a miracle that he got through the six weeks without getting his facial features altered. We had all with the exception of one man been in the services and seen drill instructors at their worst, but this man was unbelievably cruel and obnoxious, but we all wanted to be firemen so we buttoned our lips. Strangely enough the only man not to finish the course was the man who had never been in the services.

The routine was 6.30 a.m. out of bed and carry out detailed cleaning tasks in our accommodation, 7.30 a.m. breakfast, which was very wholesome, and the ladies who looked after us were magic, they looked after us like their own sons. After breakfast we got dressed in our best gear for inspection and then at 9 a.m. into the lecture rooms for lectures which went on till 12.30 p.m.

These lectures covered subjects like hydraulics, equipment, legislation, building construction and chemistry, and we took notes on all these subjects. Lunch was from

12.30 p.m. till 1.30 p.m. then on to the yard for practical drills including foot drills. This was just like being back in the services but the practical fire drills were something again, everything carried out at the double, in fact we were not allowed to walk whilst on the yard.

The hose we used had been donated to our country by the Americans during the dark days of the blitzes on our cities in the war, it was very heavy, weighing about forty to fifty pounds when it was wet. The hose also had heavy brass couplings and when you rolled up a length it would stand four foot high, and all hose drills were carried out holding the roll at shoulder height. So when the time came to pack up for the day you may have run out thirty or forty lengths of this damned stuff and, believe me, you ached across the shoulders. All the gear we used was quite old, including wartime trailer pumps for example, on leaving the school the only time you saw one of these was in a museum. As time went on we settled into a routine which seemed to make things easier, although we still got a few surprises. For example one morning per week we were roused at the normal time, told to get into our PT gear and put in the back of an old Austin lorry and taken about five or six miles up the coast round Morecambe Bay. There we were tipped out and told we would miss breakfast if we were not back in time.

After tea we would write up our lecture notes and have a question and answer session on what we had done, then you bulled up your gear ready for next morning. If after all that you had the inclination and any money you could dress in your best uniform and go into town, provided you were back in the dormitory for 11 p.m.

Some of the lads cracked it with local lassies but the best bet were the lassies on holiday. They had a bob or two and would usually buy you a pint. I think this must have been the first steps to equal rights because in those days it was usually the man who paid.

During the first six weeks of training there were a great number of minor injuries like pulled muscles and bad bruising but this was not surprising considering we were chased from pillar to post on that station yard. Five o'clock could never come around quick enough, when we could go and get a hot shower to ease some of the aches and pains.

The last Friday of the six weeks arrived and we were given oral and practical tests to perform, and in the afternoon we were informed individually of our progress on the school. I was happy with my progress with the exception of the subject of hydraulics, a subject that was to bug me for the whole of my career.

Monday saw me back at my designated station and assigned to a permanent watch, 'White', with Stn O Gilmour in charge. Once again I was put on the Pump/Escape under his watchful eye, but this time in the event of a turn out I was to become involved as a member of the team. After parade we did a couple of drills using lightweight hose, which was a doddle compared to the stuff used at training school.

During the next few weeks we turned out several times but to nothing spectacular; being a rookie I wanted every turn out to be something out of the ordinary. I got to know all the lads on the watch and without exception every one was so helpful, nothing was too much trouble for them, they would spend ages with me watching me practice knots and lines, a subject which I eventually prided myself on. I managed to keep out of trouble during this period of time and applied myself to reading the Fire Service manuals whenever we were on stand down.

We had a TV on the station but it was about the size of a postage stamp and it was very rarely used, cribbage was one of the most popular card games played when on stand down.

It was during this period my fiancée and I set our wedding date, so we started to look around at property and finally settled for a two-bed terraced house near my parents and two miles from the fire station. It cost four hundred and fifty pounds, so I borrowed fifty pound deposit from my parents and the rest was to be paid off at a pound a week plus interest, but still the main thing was that we would not be starting life under my parents' roof, which in those days was usually the done thing in the early days of a marriage. The big day was to be the second Saturday after I finished my second spell at training school.

The weeks seemed to flash by and it was time to go back to Morecambe. We all met up again and I think we all tried to outdo one another with stories of the shouts that we had attended on our stations, but soon it was back to the same old routine. This time we would spend one week on learning about and wearing breathing apparatus.

Being ex-servicemen we all knew the secret of putting a shine on our boots and shoes, but I must admit it was a bit frustrating to bull up your fire boots for parade only to have them scratched to hell whilst carrying out drills after the parade. We got a second pair of fire boots issued after our training so we were always able to keep one pair in a good state, but that was no excuse for dirty boots on your next parade. The electric iron and toothbrush handles got a lot of use, we used these to smooth out the wrinkles in the boots, the other method was to coat the boots with a thick layer of boot polish and then light it, the idea being that this method put a nice layer of polish over the leather ready for the spit and polish.

During this second six weeks we spent a lot of time doing rehearsals of a set number of drills that would be performed for the chief officer and his senior officers who would be attending the passing out parade. These were going like clockwork but our instructor was always trying to get us to knock seconds off running up an escape ladder, or getting a jet to work from a pump.

One of the most demanding drills was the simulated rescue where you carried a colleague down a fifty-five foot escape ladder from the drill tower – when you had done this drill for the first couple of times the backs of your calf and thigh muscles screamed at you.

Another of the drills we did was to get a one-inch diameter jet to work at a pressure of one hundred pounds per square inch. This we were told was the equivalent of trying to hold a twelve-stone man pushing up and backwards at the same time. A lot of skill and strength was required to stop the jet from getting away from you, and on the occasions it did. The whole length of hose, with a brass branchpipe attached would whip about like a demented snake. The pump operator had to be on the lookout at all times for firemen losing control of the branch, and he had to close down the pump or delivery very rapidly.

Another drill I used to enjoy was the Hook Ladders. Whilst a lot of the lads did not look forward to them I found them to be a great challenge. The ladder was made of wood, thirteen feet long and weighing between twenty-five and thirty pounds, at the top it had a high tensile steel serrated hook. The idea being that you could scale the face of a building via the window sills; you smashed the hook through the window and the hook went over the sill and your weight on the ladder kept it in position. Then you scaled the ladder, straddled the sill, and then smashed the ladder through the next window above, and so on until you reached the required window. I never saw them used in anger, but I believe in the early days of their introduction a good few rescues had been carried out using them.

All went well, then it was on to our breathing apparatus training, after a very comprehensive theory course we started to wear them. In those days the sets you wore contained pure oxygen, which you breathed through a mouthpiece whilst wearing a nose clip. We trained on two types: the Salvus set, which contained enough oxygen for thirty minutes, and the Proto, which would last for one hour.

All the practical drills took place in an old air raid shelter that was filled with all types of obstacles and inside were several old type braziers in which coke fires were kept going full blast. During drills wet cardboard would be put on the fires which in turn managed to generate lots of thick heavy smoke. We went in working in pairs to locate a dummy that we thought weighed fifteen stone and fetch out the same. During this training we were taught how to use the entrapped procedure – in the event of getting trapped you were to sit down and relax and, by means of a bypass valve, keep inflating the bag on the set and breath the oxygen from the bag. We were assured that a one hour set could last you up to eight hours using this set up, but I thank the Lord I was never called upon to test this theory.

After successfully passing this part of the course we were all given a certificate of competency in the use of breathing apparatus, then back to prepare for our passing out display, which as you would expect went off without a hitch. Considering the amount of rehearsal hours this was hardly surprising. Afterwards we got the usual sort of pep talk you would expect in the circumstances, this was followed by a talk from the course commandant who told us how we were by far the best course to have passed through his school, but at that moment every one of us would have believed anything he said. We were that glad it was all over, no more running round silly coastlines in the early hours, although to be honest I am sure we were all a damn sight fitter than we were before we commenced our training.

That evening we adjourned to a local pub where refreshments, liquid and other, had been laid on from the five bob a week that we had contributed from the start of our second six weeks. We had a good evening and even Sub O Bastard was allowed in the company.

The following morning we said our farewells and set off to our own stations to stow our gear and to find out when to report for duty with our watches, in my case Monday morning.

Probation and Operational

That weekend I was running around getting things arranged for the wedding which was to take place in a small village in Cheshire. My future in-laws had everything under control concerning the reception, which was to be held in the local village hall. My main problem was getting a bus arranged to transport my side of the family the twenty-eight miles to the village, but I eventually solved that problem.

After roll call on the Monday morning I was taken into the station office where I was promptly read the riot act by Stn O Gilmour. 'If you don't pull your weight I will have your guts for garters and any misbehaviour and you will be up the road.'

I came out of that office thinking I have done nothing wrong and I have had a rollicking, what will it be like if I ever really do something wrong. Very fortunately I never had to find out. It was then I realised I had forgotten to request time off for my marriage, so back in I went and made my request. Instead of jumping at me he did quite the opposite, he phoned Brigade HQ and they allowed me to take two Bank Holidays in lieu, which meant in actual fact that I owed the Brigade two days.

The Stn O really was just a big pussy cat, and so I got married on the Saturday and went on nights on the Monday.

On the Saturday night of the wedding we returned to our new home but unfortunately so did ten of the guests and half of them decided to bed down on the settee and chairs for the night, so it was about three thirty in the morning before my new bride and I retired to bed. Then my wife decided to get up and cook breakfast for the people who had stayed over, but eventually we got them all away about eleven in the morning. So I said, 'Right, let's go back to bed for a while', after all it was my wedding weekend. Anyway off we went upstairs to bed but within ten minutes there was a knocking on the front door which we ignored until I heard my mother shout up, so downstairs I went and let her and my aunt in. They had brought some wedding presents over, so I gave up the idea of bed until night time. I had a wonderful honeymoon.

The working week consisted of a sixty-hour week; a week of days 9 a.m. till 6 p.m., followed by a week of nights 6 p.m. till 9 a.m. the next day. We got two days a week off which were progressive, Tuesday and Wednesday one week followed by Wednesday and Thursday the following week and so on, with Saturday being the changeover from day duty to nights. Now the bad thing about this was if you were off Thursday and Friday on days, you then went back at 9 a.m. Saturday until 9 a.m. Sunday morning and then back on at 6 p.m. Sunday night, which meant that particular week you worked a ninety-nine-hour week, but this was the life I had chosen so I just got on with it.

The day came quite soon when I was involved with my first fatality. We received a call to a house on fire in the afternoon, when we got there we were informed a man who was an invalid was in the house but he slept downstairs. I was ordered to put on BA with the leading fireman and in we went with a small jet; a quick splash around to quieten the fire, and then we commenced to search around in the smoke. I found a bed in the corner but there was no one on it, so following the procedure we had been taught I went on my knees to feel around and under the bed. I put my hand on the body and with the aid of my lamp I had a look – it was not a pretty sight. I signalled to my partner that I had found the body, he had a look and signalled to leave it where it was and to go out.

When we got outside I told the officer we had found the body but it was dead and we had left it alone. He promptly asked me if I was a doctor. I thought he had gone loopy or something, but I replied no to his question, and he then explained that only a doctor could confirm if a person was dead or not. That particular conversation stayed with me.

I did not feel in the least upset having found the body, but I saw many a man shaking after his first encounter with a dead person. The man had apparently been smoking in bed and ignited the bedding having dozed off, he must have woken up and rolled out of the bed before being overcome by smoke, the burning bedding had done the rest. It was amazing the number of incidents that I attended over the years where the cause was attributed to smoking in bed.

One morning we went on duty and the night shift related a story that we all thought was quite funny. They had been called out on a make up in Manchester's area in support of crews already attending at the large zoological gardens and amusement park in which was situated a large ballroom, which was well alight. When the crew arrived they were detailed to put a water screen over the building which housed the big cats. They got this organised and in the meantime the lions and tigers were roaring and very unsettled due to the noise and the goings on. After about half an hour the sub officer in charge decided to check round the back of the building, and according to the other lads he came shooting back as white as a ghost and saying there was a lion at the back that had escaped. He went off to find a zoo official to report this to and he eventually found a keeper who came back with him and he asked the sub to show him where he had seen the beast. He very reluctantly went round the back to show him, and a few minutes later a very sheepish sub came back. The lion turned out to be a donkey which was tethered in a corner of a children's play area. It was a long time before he lived that down but as he said with the big cats roaring, he really was convinced one was loose.

It was shortly after this that I came home from work one morning to find a neighbour waiting for me, she said that she had not seen our next door neighbour for over twenty-four hours, and that all the doors were locked. I climbed over the back yard wall and looked through the kitchen window and saw a man lying on the floor near the cooker. I told the lady to call the police and an ambulance and then I broke in via the back door. On entering I was hit by the strong smell of gas, which in those days was coal gas not the natural gas of today that has no smell. I turned off the gas at the meter and then grabbed hold of the man, my intention being to drag him outside and to perform artificial respiration on him, but when I got hold of him he was like a plank with rigor mortis. What struck me most was the colour of the man, it was a delicate shade of pink.

Shortly afterwards the police and ambulance arrived and contacted a local doctor who came and said life was extinct and the man had been dead for at least eighteen hours. Whilst all this was going on a police inspector arrived. As he sat down and pulled out his cigarettes, I said, 'If you intend to light that I am off.' The house still reeked of gas.

He said, 'I was not thinking.'

The outcome at the inquest was that the man had been made redundant from a cotton mill where he had worked since he was thirteen and he was sixty-two when he committed suicide, so rather than being able to put to good use the first aid I had been taught I found myself at a coroner's inquest.

A few days later I encountered a situation where experience certainly counted. We were called in the early hours to a big old house that was being used by winos and down and outs. When we got there the fire had got into the roof void, Bill and I were detailed to check the upper floors for anyone still in the building. Whilst on the uppermost floor I heard Bill shout, 'Look out', and off he went whilst I was knocked to my knees in lath and big lumps of ornamental plaster.

Bill came and dragged me out onto a landing and when I had recovered I asked him how the hell he knew that lot was going to fall. His answer was that he had heard the creaks; I had heard damn all and if I had have done I doubt if I could have beaten Bill out of the room and he was twenty-five years older than me.

A sad thing happened a few days after that. Bill sat in his chair at home to await his evening meal and passed away. He was less than five years away from his retirement.

A few days after this I was offered my first part-time job, helping a furniture remover on his van. Now whilst part-time work was officially forbidden, everyone did it to supplement their income, so off I went on my days off. The work was heavy and not well paid but I did manage to obtain a few bargains in the second-hand furniture line so slowly my little house became nice and cosy.

Then my wife obtained employment in a local factory as a packer, so our income was steadily improving and we were able to go out with a couple of friends most weekends when I was off duty.

I had by this time started to play soccer on a regular basis for our local team, in those days we did not get paid overtime but got time off in lieu. I used to save my time till I had enough to have three hours off on a Saturday to enable me to play, and also I was getting invites to play for

Manchester fire brigade in their Wednesday league games when they were short of a goalkeeper.

It was here that I met the lad who was to become my lifelong friend, his name was Brian but due to his shock of red hair was known always as Ginge. He had a party trick which used to drive me mad, if we were winning say three nil towards the end of a match he would deliberately shove a pass back past me into the net, something the opposition had not managed to do all afternoon. He would then swear blind it was a accident. I was to get to know him even better as the years went on.

It was rarely we went on duty without a least one bell which broke the hours up nicely, but the busiest night of the year was Bonfire Night. It was a case of in and out of the station all night, but in those days the children did not throw stones at you like they do today; firemen drew a lot of respect from the public then. Most people seemed to think a fireman could do most things and could be relied upon at any time.

One Thursday night we received a call in the early hours of the morning to a rag warehouse in Oldham's area, this was called a make up, when the officer in charge needs more men and appliances to fight a fire. Off we went to find one half of an old railway warehouse well alight at one end, our crew were detailed to pull down these bales of rags to allow crews to attack the fire behind them.

Whilst we were doing this, rats the size of ruddy Corgi dogs were running and scampering past us. When we were finally relieved and allowed to go back to our station we showered and went home, and I went to bed to wake up about three o'clock feeling terrible just like a bad dose of flue coming on, but it was our last night on and that would give me a full day to shake it off.

So on duty I went and early in the evening we got a call to a bedroom fire with a flock mattress throwing off the normal heavy smoke. After this was out we went back to the station and I could not stop shaking and sweating, the station officer told me to get off home, which I did and went straight to bed. Early the next morning my wife went round to tell my mother I was ill and around she came and decided to call a doctor, I can remember his arriving and talking to me, he did not say what he thought it might be but he said he would be back at five o'clock.

In the meantime my limbs started to go numb and my eyesight started to blur, the next thing I remember was waking up in hospital on a Wednesday morning to see my wife sat at my bedside where I learned later she had been since my admittance to hospital on the Saturday.

My wife told me that they thought I was suffering from polio or meningitis but whatever it was I could not come to terms with the fact I could not move or feel my legs. Later that day a doctor came to talk to me and one of the questions he asked was had I recently been in contact with rats or mice. When I related to him about the rag warehouse he said that confirmed what the blood tests were showing and that I had contracted Weill's disease, a disease spread by being in contact with the urine of rats and mice. It was easy to understand how it had happened, we had been perspiring heavily and the natural tendency to wipe your face with your hand had obviously passed the germs onto my lips and bingo there it was.

It was three weeks before I was able to move my limbs fully again and during those weeks I certainly prayed, although I cannot say that I was a particularly religious person. I visualised myself in a wheelchair and not being able to participate in sports again, my mind just ran riot lying there.

During this period in hospital my wife was asked if she would go to the station to collect my wages, she had no idea I got paid when I was off sick. I was off for another six weeks before I was allowed to go back on operational duties, and to this day I will run a bloody mile if I see rats or mice.

It was not long before I did my first solo watchroom duty, and a very daunting experience it turned out to be. Besides there being a small internal switchboard there was a bright red telephone on which all fire calls were received from the telephone exchange. This phone had a very shrill ring and whenever it rang it made me jump, particularly in the early hours of the morning,

On receipt of a fire call you flicked on the emergency lights and took down the address in triplicate on a standard form, one copy for the officer of each appliance. When you had taken the address you looked it up in a big book called the *Street Schedule* this told you what appliances to send to a particular risk. By the time you had done this, the duty leading fireman would have arrived to collect the address forms, you put the bells down, which rang for a predetermined time, then when the appliances had been dispatched you had to ring brigade control and inform them of the turn out. We did not yet have radios on the machines so all communications were by telephone, out on the fireground the officer in charge would send back messages by telephone, which the dutyman in turn relayed to control. We used a codeword to the operator so we did not have to pay although each appliance had a tin with a number of pennies in so that they could use a telephone for non-emergencies. I went to several mill fires over the next few weeks. Whilst they were usually difficult to locate in the heavy smoke and invariably breathing apparatus had to be used, you did get used to breathing in smoke, one of the secrets was not to panic and start to gasp for breath – that was the quickest way to finish up on your back.

Watching the old hands was the way to learn, there was always something they could show you, and you would have been a fool to ignore their advice. Whilst they might take the mickey out of you on the station, on the fireground it became serious, no pranks.

It was not long before I had my first prank played on me. We went to a chimney fire one evening. When we were ready to come home I was detailed to watch the driver reverse into a side street, which I did and he promptly shot off and left me. I had no option but to jump on a trolley bus in my fire gear and explain to the conductor what had happened as I had no money for my fare. He waived the fare, but when I got back to the station the boss said, 'Where the hell have you been?' as if he did not know!

One day we got called to a man trapped under a bus very near the station. When we released him he was in a critical condition. Now nearby was a Catholic church and someone must have told the priest who came across and leaned over the victim and we all heard him say quite plainly, 'Are you of the faith, my son?' This upset one of the older members of the crew who told the priest to clear off saying what the hell does it matter what religion he is, he is in a very serious state you should minister to him and comfort him. The priest started to burble on but the ambulance arrived and the casualty was taken away where he succumbed to his injuries in hospital.

Christmas week, 1956 saw me posing as Father Christmas, being the junior man of the watch. I dressed in all the regalia and got on the roof of the town hall. All the children and their parents were gathered in the square. At a given moment a spotlight was shone on me and the commentator told the children I was stuck on the roof. 'What shall we do?' a cry went up. 'Send for the fire brigade', and around the corner came the turntable ladder, lights flashing and bells ringing. I was lowered down in the slings and after giving out presents we adjourned to the mayor's parlour, where I was given a couple of nips of the good stuff.

Another incident which left me rather embarrassed was shortly to occur. The dormitory was fitted with two-tier steel bunks, which had a diamond pattern of steel springs. Being the newest member of the watch I was allocated a top bunk. You were issued with three small mattresses filled with horsehair. One particular night we all turned in and in the early hours I awoke with a tremendous pain in my left leg. Now I had a terrible habit of sleeping on my stomach and when I woke up I could not turn over. With great difficulty I managed to reach the bedding on the next bed and I pulled the bedding until Vic whose bed it was woke up and asked what the hell I was doing. I told him I was stuck. His answer was not to be so bloody daft and get back to sleep. By this time some of the other lads heard this and one got up and brought a lamp off the appliance, pulled back my blankets and laughingly announced, 'Your toe is stuck in the spring.'

By this time I really was in agony so someone brought the bolt croppers off the appliance and nipped the steel spring, for a moment I flaked out with the pain. They pulled my sock off and burst out laughing as my toe was the size and colour of an overripe Victoria plum. What had happened was that I had turned on my stomach and gone to sleep and my toe had become wedged in the end of the diamond-shaped spring, cutting off the circulation, which caused my toe to swell. It took an awful long time to live that one down.

It was about this time that my wife and I decided to try for a family, and a few months later she announced she was pregnant. This sent the in-laws into a flutter as it would be their first grandchild.

It was shortly after this that I was called into the office to get my second six monthly probation report. When my boss had finished reading it out he asked me if I agreed with it which I did and so I signed it. He had quite a long chat with me about how I should think about bettering myself once I was through my probation but that was still a long time away but I could still prepare myself for the exams by doing a bit of studying at nights when on duty. He was a very fair man and in my humble opinion a first-class fire officer who looked after his men.

The months went by and before I realised it, I was daddy of a baby daughter which arrived whilst I was on night duty. I went straight to the hospital when I came off duty, and they were both first class, we decided on the name Sylvia Denise there and then.

It was not long before I got my first real taste of heat. We got a call to a make up in Oldham's area to a cotton mill. The first thing we saw as we arrived was a BA man being carried out by two other BA men. It turned out that this man had been overcome with heat exhaustion. The fire was in the basement of a mill and the fire was in cotton bales that had been broken open ready for combing out. It was giving off a tremendous amount of heat and thick black smoke. It was a case of taking what you could then getting to hell out of it before you became overcome. It took over two hours to get in and contain the fire, then a long while longer to drag out all the loose cotton and damp it down.

My probation period seemed to flash past and soon I was called before the divisional officer to be informed that I had successfully passed my probation and I was now a fireman with still lots to learn and again that little nudge, pass your exams and aim for higher things.

A Qualified Fireman

Nineteen fifty-eight arrived and I sat and passed both parts of my leading fireman's examination, now I was on my way or so I thought.

Shortly after this a vacancy was advertised for a L/Fm at another station in the brigade, I cheekily applied for it and actually got an interview but with my length of service I stood no chance but nevertheless nothing, ventured nothing gained. I was told not to be deterred because I had not got it, but in the years to come I found it to be for the best.

Snotty-nosed youngsters getting promoted so early in their service left a lot to be desired, nothing replaced experience and the older hands left you in no doubt as to that. In years to come I saw and experienced some of these so called whizkids most of whom were a pain in the bum. Ask them anything from the book and they could tell you, but on the fireground a lot of these officers were sheer rubbish who would come and ask your advice on certain procedures. There is an awful lot to be said for experience.

A few days later four of us were nominated to go on a course to Moreton-in-Marsh, which was in Gloucestershire. It was called Emergency Water Scheme and it was for procedures to be implemented in the event of another war.

We travelled down in a Green Goddess driven by our leading fireman, stopping at various fire stations en route to fill up with petrol. Moreton was an old wartime RAF airfield and not a great deal had changed, with old Nissan huts being our place of accommodation with great pot-bellied stoves to heat the hut. This place was eventually to become the Fire Service College and when I went back there a good number of years after it was like going into a first-class hotel, the transformation was phenomenal.

For the whole of the week we were there it rained cats and dogs and we were up to our knees in reddish coloured mud. The only place we could dry our gear was on chairs placed around the stove, so you went to bed and slept in a damp fug.

On the last evening there, I came back from my evening meal in the mess to find some lads from a midland brigade playing brag in the hut. I watched for a short time, and having a few bob in my pocket I asked if I could join in. Now if ever Lady Luck sat on my shoulder she did that evening. After the first couple of hands I was dealt the top hand, a prile of threes. Now other members of the school had reasonable hands, with just coppers left and only two of us left in, the other lad decided to see me but as he only had a prile of kings I scooped the kitty. I played till nine o'clock and finished up eleven pounds up. I had never had luck like that before, so I went off to buy my mates a few beers each in the bar.

Towards the middle of 1959 I thought it was time to broaden my horizons and move on to another brigade for different types of experience, and so I wrote to an East Anglian brigade to see if they had any vacancies. An interview was arranged and away I went; with hindsight I should have done this differently I should have informed my brigade first of my intentions but there it was. The Anglian brigade agreed to my transfer if it was okay with my brigade, so back I went and requested a transfer. I was interviewed by the deputy chief who left me in no doubt what he thought of my request. He asked me why I wanted to move and I told him to gain rural experience etc. He offered to post me to a rural area in this brigade if that was what I wanted, but having already put the wheels in motion I decided to carry on with the request for a transfer. Anyhow he agreed to let me transfer, so then began the rush to organise things such as the sale of my house. I was due to start in my new brigade in three weeks' time, and a week after putting the house on the market we got a buyer at a reasonable profit. All that remained now was for me to get us fixed up at our new destination. In the meantime my wife announced she was pregnant again, but that was no problem as we wanted another child anyhow.

I decided to have a farewell leaving do on my last Saturday with the brigade, and it worked out just right as our watch came off nights on the Saturday morning. We held the do in our local pub and a great deal of ale was consumed. I was told a number of times that night that I was making a big mistake in leaving the County, and how right that turned out to be.

Next morning we went on duty and there were a few fragile firemen who sat in the canteen after checking the appliances. At about 11.30 a.m. the bells went down to attend a fire in a railway warehouse, as we turned out of the gates we could see the thick black cloud of smoke.

It was a warehouse of five floors and the top three floors were well alight, so the officer in charge asked for twenty pumps to attend. I was on the turntable ladder so within minutes of arriving I was way above the roof pouring water into the building, whilst I was up there the roof collapsed and the blast of heat which hit me took my breath away. We spent the rest of the day at that incident till we were relieved in the evening, and so I finished my service with the County.

The Nightmare

I travelled down to my new brigade on the Monday leaving my family behind until I could arrange some accommodation for us all. I was given two days off to let me look around for digs and with the help of a civilian clerk from the town hall I rented a furnished room from a very elderly lady. This would suffice till we could find our own place, and so I sent for my family to join me.

My very first tour of duty should have prepared me for what I had let myself in for, the gear on the appliance was so old, with unlined hose, the appliance itself was quite ancient and they had a sixty-foot hand-operated turntable ladder the likes of which I had never seen before. Just to make matters worse, on my first day we went to the canteen and I sat on the first chair I came to when the eldest member of the watch walked in and told me that I was in his chair, I jokingly picked it up, looked underneath and said, 'I don't see your name on it.' Oh my goodness, he ranted and raved about new interlopers coming and taking over. I cannot ever remember that man's speaking a civil word to me for the rest of my service there, so I really did not get off to a good start.

It was almost six weeks before I heard the bells in anger, and we turned out to a grass fire on a railway embankment.

In the meantime we found a builder who had some plots for sale about three miles up the coast right on the seafront. We had sufficient money to buy a plot and arranged to have a two-bed detached bungalow built. The price was three thousand seven hundred and fifty pounds, and I didn't have a problem getting a mortgage. A few years ago my wife and I attended a wedding down there and we went to see our old bungalow, and the asking price for the same type of bungalow was one hundred and twenty five thousand pounds.

The old lady we stayed with was the top dog of the WRVS and I am sure she was still living through the war years. She would not throw away a can, jar or a sheet of newspaper, everything was stored in a shed in her garden. It was a veritable Aladdin's cave, but we got along together, me doing odd jobs around this big old house of hers.

The worst part about it was that the house was overrun with vermin, and with my past illness in mind I told her of the dangers of this, but they did not worry her. I am sure she treated them like pets as we would hear her talking to the damn things.

One day whilst she was out I went into the attic and the floor was strewn with pears and all of them had been gnawed. When she came home I showed her the situation and she said she would attend to it. Now unknown to us she placed rat poison all over the place, and a couple of weeks later when I came off night duty I found the house pervaded with the most awful stench. I lifted a couple of floorboards where the smell was strongest and there I found a bloated decomposing rat and several small mice. I fetched the lady in to show her and she was appalled, she straight away fetched in a local firm, which went through the house lifting floorboards and removing the dead vermin.

It was whilst we lived here my son was born in the local hospital, and very shortly after we moved into our new home. We were so desperate to move in, the plaster had still not dried out on the walls. I had by this time found myself a part-time job as a barman in a local pub so with the extra income I bought a moped to enable me to get to and from work a lot easier and quicker.

It was about now that my other hobby became useful. I like fishing so when I wasn't working part time I would go down to the beach and fish for cod or whiting. This made a nice meal for us.

The situation at work went from bad to worse, same old routine, very few calls and the boredom starting to get to me. The lads on the watch reckoned the lads in the city had to turn out all the time and here we were living the life of Riley and getting paid the same money as them.

A rather funny thing happened in the summer, the brigade had the Home Office inspector to do his annual visit, and we all paraded in our best gear and he proceeded to inspect the crew. When the test turn out was called for the pump responded and the sliding doors were then pushed back the other way for the turntable ladder to turn out. Unfortunately the doors jammed on the runners, so the turntable ladder was unable to turn out until the doors were lifted up back onto the runners by council workmen, it was not a very good start to the Home Office inspection.

Early next holiday season I obtained a job calling bingo numbers on the pleasure beach. A lad from another watch and I worked it between us it was easy and the pay was not too bad. During the summer months there was no shortage of visitors, who came to stay a week or so with us, so my wife and children were not short of company at that time.

In the autumn one of the lads who owned a small boat asked me if I would like to go out night fishing with him for cod, I said I would, so at nine o'clock we pushed the boat off the beach and proceeded out about a mile or so offshore to the 'Scroby Sands' where we caught loads of cod, up to twenty pounds in weight. When we came ashore he gave me a share of the catch, so after I had taken a couple for my own table, I took the rest to the local fish and chip shop the following day and the owner paid me the princely sum of one and six a pound (eight pence) for the rest. So apart from enjoying the fishing I made a bob or two.

Meanwhile things at the station got no better, same old routines and drills, never any variation in drills. The majority of the lads at the station were on there last few years of service, most of them being ex-National Fire Service personnel from the war years, so they were quite happy to come on duty and never turn out, they thought I was mad and perhaps in a way they were right. It was whilst I was in this brigade I got caught up in active union work. We had one substation in this brigade and the union official served at it. There was no one in the main station, nobody seemed bothered about the union, they were all wrapped up in their own little world.

The outcome was that I became the union rep for the station, and my first task was to get the men on the station to join as no one was bothered about the union. I managed to recruit seventy-five per cent of the station personnel but they were never what one would call committed members, they were happy to plod along with the outdated equipment and conditions. There were still no drying facilities available, not that we had much use for them as we never seemed to turn out enough to get wet.

The biggest risk the brigade had was a life risk in the summer months when the population rose with the influx of holidaymakers, apart from that there was very little industrial risk.

Every year the horse race meeting was held at a course just outside the town, and when these were in progress a man was detailed off every tour of duty to attend the course where they placed four lengths of hose and a standpipe and a branchpipe; this was to be used in the event of a fire in the stables. When on day duty you were given a few shillings out of petty cash, this was to cover the cost of a meal, but anyone who has ever attended a race course will know what they charge for a meal, what we got would hardly cover the price of a Kit-Kat, but at least it was something different.

Come 1960 my morale was at rock bottom and I finally snapped when at last we got a call to something other than grass fires. We got a call to a fire on a coastal tanker in a dry dock. When we arrived we were informed that there was a fire in the engine room. Myself and a leading fireman were told to put on BA sets and go down, when we got down the first companionway I realised it was cold smoke with no heat to be felt. When we got to the entrance to the engine room the other lad said he had a problem with his set, these were the old thirty-minute Salvus sets, according to the rules I should have accompanied him back but I was so close to the fire I decided to carry on.

It was only a couple of yards farther on when I found a few oily cleaning rags smouldering on a grating, so I gave them a good soaking and gathered up a few of them and made my way out. The smoke had virtually dissipated by then.

When I got back on the deck the chief officer was there so I told him that the fires were out and that all it was was a few rags. At this I thought he was going to have a fit, yelling, 'Who are you to tell me that the fire is out?' He ordered me to put on another set and go below and give it a good soaking. That was the straw that broke the camel's back, I put on another set, which was not really necessary as the smoke had almost gone but I went down the companionway and sat down, after about twenty minutes or so two more BA men came down to look for me, so back up I went but before he could start up again and say too much I ripped into him verbally and told him what he could do with his bloody Fred Karnos brigade. He just said, 'I will see you in my office when you get back to the station.' On my way back I thought I had blown it but I didn't care.

I was called into his office and for the first time in my short career I was facing a man for whom I had no respect for whatsoever. He had tried to humiliate me on the deck of that tanker, and before he could say anything I told him to charge me if he wanted but that I would not be there to answer it as I was resigning. He then told me to calm down and to think about what I was saying, as I had a family to support and no other job to go to, but my mind was made up, his last words in my ears as I left the office were, 'Don't think I will ever give you a reference for another job.' I turned round and told him he was not a fit man to write a reference for anyone.

I sat and wrote out my resignation which was to take effect in four weeks' time.

On my arrival home I had to explain to my wife what I had done. She said she had been expecting something like this to happen for a while as she had seen what was happening to me. Then she asked what were we going to do now, I told her we would go back up to the North West and I would find a job and somewhere to live.

Back to Square One

I applied to join Cheshire County Police, but without a reference from my last employer they did not want to know.

Whilst I had been working the bingo I had traded in my moped for a second-hand 350cc motorcycle so on the bike I went on my days off to find a job and somewhere to stay.

Now this is where I began to believe in miracles.

I stayed with my mother-in-law in Cheshire whilst I looked for a job, which I quickly obtained at ICI as a process worker. Now my mother-in-law was a rather canny lady and when her daughter and I got engaged she had put our names on the local authority housing list.

She told me to go and see what the prospects were for a house, and I took myself off to the housing office at the town hall and was shown into a office to be interviewed by a lady. I told the lady my wife's maiden name and that we had put our names on the list, she then said there was already a letter in the post to my wife's premarital home offering us a tenancy of a two-bed house in the village where my in-laws lived and did I want to accept it.

I did not tell her of our situation but I was prepared to accept the house which was in a quiet cul-de-sac near my mother-in-law. Sure enough next day a letter arrived and I accepted the tenancy, then it was back on the bike and back home to break the news to my good lady wife, who like me then began to believe in miracles.

We put the bungalow on the market and within ten days I had a buyer at the asking price, which gave me a good bit of profit, then I went back to work out my notice, the lads could not believe I had a job and a new home in such a short time. There were no farewells this time from the brigade but it was like a ton weight off my shoulders. Whilst the lads in general were fine the senior staff left an awful lot to be desired in their attitude.

So we moved back to Cheshire and the job I was doing paid me the sort of wages I had only dreamt about before, and before long I traded in my bike for a Heinkel bubble car so now I was able to take the family out. However, it did not take long for me to start wondering if I could get back into the brigade.

Early 1961 saw me discuss with my wife whether I should apply, and with her backing I wrote to Manchester fire brigade and asked if there were any vacancies. Within two weeks I received the application forms which I filled in and returned also enclosing a letter explaining the reason I had left my last position in East Anglia. It was not too long before I was requested to attend for a interview on a Saturday morning at London Road fire station in Manchester.

A Second Chance

On reporting at the training school, I found several other hopeful candidates. The format was similar to my very first interview apart from the questions I was asked regarding the circumstances of my resignation of my last position. I did not endeavour to cover anything up and told them a lot of it had to do with sheer boredom and frustration and as regarding the blow-up on the tanker fire, I said that in my five years in the RAF and my previous fire service career, I had never been spoken to by anyone as I had been spoken to by a chief officer, who had no idea of the situation down below in that tanker's engine room.

I was asked if I normally let my temper get the better of me and I answered with an emphatic no, I also told them of the threat of never getting a reference from him, but the senior officer on the panel just asked if I could produce my service discharge book and another name as a referee, which I said I could. I was sent out for a medical and after that down to the station yard for the obligatory fireman's carry.

We were then told that we would be informed in due course whether we had been successful in our applications. I went back feeling a little optimistic but even if I did not get a position I still had a job and a house. It was about a further two weeks before I got a letter to say that I had been accepted and that I was to report to the training school at London Road on a Monday in a couple of weeks' time and to confirm if I would be attending, the speed with which I wrote back to confirm this was no one's business.

Off I went on the appointed date to meet up with twenty-odd other recruits and to be addressed by Mr Cassidy, our course commandant. After being split up into groups and introduced to our instructors, we were taken to collect our equipment. Other members of the course came from other brigades throughout the country. We also a Sheikh's son from one of the oil states of the Arab Emirates. He was to eventually go back as a officer at one of the refineries. This chap got a monthly allowance from home which was much more than our annual wages and whenever he went out, it was with a dolly bird on his arm, but he was actually quite funny and found the course hard going.

In contrast to my first training course we were to do twelve weeks straight off and if I had thought my first training sessions were tough they were nothing compared to The City of Manchester's training course. To start with we were under the eye of all the senior officers of the brigade, London Road being the headquarters station.

The building itself was in the shape of a huge triangle and four floors high. One side housed the operational department, which included seven fire appliances, the canteen and dormitory for the operational personnel and the two floors above were occupied as married quarters. On the other side was the club room and gymnasium, recruits' accommodation, lecture room, a laundry, single firemen's quarters and again married quarters but also on the ground floor was a police station and cells. In the corner was the drill tower, the base of the triangle was formed by, on the ground floor and basement, the brigade control room. The first floor consisted of staff offices and the fire prevention department plus married quarters and the second and third floors were also married quarters.

After being issued with our gear we went into the lecture room where we were left in no doubt as to our fate if we failed to come up to the standards required of us. No one had yet commented on my having been in the brigade although Mr Cassidy had been on the panel that interviewed me, so once again it was back to bulling your fire gear and best shoes.

On the Tuesday training began in earnest with PT being taken by a sub officer who had represented Great Britain in the Berlin Olympics, I think it was as a weightlifter; what was easy to him was agony to us.

A trick I never mastered was climbing the ropes which let down from the gym ceiling; after the PT session it was breakfast followed by lectures, after lunch it was down on the yard for drills.

In the beginning it was funny to watch some of the lads who had never been servicemen marching with left arm and left foot working together and being told they were marching like a bunch of pregnant penguins (today I suppose that would be classed as abuse, particularly if you had a firewoman on the course) but they were soon whipped into shape.

It was on the yard which was made of red terracotta tiles, I witnessed more spectacular falls than I thought possible, when wet this surface was treacherous, but it did not take long for the lads to get the hang of staying upright. For four weeks I carried on the school till one lunch time I was told to report to Mr Cassidy's office, which I did fearing the worst, but all he said to me was to be dressed in my best gear for two o'clock and be outside his office. All through lunch I kept trying to think had I done anything wrong but nothing would come to mind. Deputy chief's office – this could only mean the boot.

In I marched to stand face to face with the man second only to God in this brigade. He asked me if I had any idea why I was there and I answered no. 'Well,' he said, 'Mr Cassidy tells me it is a waste of time for you to continue on the training school as you know all the basics so all that you are doing is repetition. So as from Monday you will report to Stn Officer Williams on White watch at London Road for operational duties and good luck.'

This was just unbelievable news, I spent the rest of the afternoon in a dream and packing up my gear. When the lads came off the yard they thought I had got the push but I finally convinced them I was going operational. Well I was a lucky bastard and lots more things as well but the fact remained I had finished at the school.

I took myself off home and told my wife the good news, it was then for the first and only time she really attempted to lecture me on how I had been given this chance and not to blow it this time, a promise I was to keep.

On the Monday I reported for duty and the first person I bumped into was my old footballing pal Ginge, he showed me the locker room and put me right about the oncoming watch parade.

The parade of oncoming and offgoing watches at London Road took place on the station yard, and in the married quarters lived the third senior officer of the brigade who used to watch the parade from behind the lace curtains of his flat, and woe betide the officer in charge of the parade if it was not carried out to his satisfaction.

After I paraded, my name had not been read out for an appliance so I spoke to the duty leading fireman who said the boss wanted to see me first. So off I went to the station office to be confronted by Station Officer Williams, I was told to stand to attention then he began, 'I have seen your record and I am not impressed, try anything funny or out of order on my watch and you are up the bloody road. I see you are married with a family, remember that, I can always get new firemen but you will not always be able to get a decent job so off you go and do your job well and you will not be bothered by me and that is the way I want it. Now out you go and show us all what you are capable of doing when required.'

I came out of that office thinking I had heard something similar to that from a Mr Gilmour a few years ago, anyhow I was told to put my gear on the salvage tender, this was the crew who were responsible for salvage work after a fire, covering stock with salvage sheets and getting rid of excess water and putting down sawdust to soak up water. Then it was on the yard to play volleyball for a half hour before we carried out situation drills.

It did not take long to get into the swing of things, there were about twenty-two officers and men on duty at any one time at London Road. These manned two pump/escapes, two turntable ladders, foam tender, emergency tender, salvage tender and two wireless cars for the duty officers.

On the first day on duty with the watch I was given my nickname by which was to become known for all my service life, being six foot tall and eleven stone four pounds it was natural that I should be christened Slim.

The pump/escapes at London Road were at that time Rolls Royce Dennis and were fitted with a thousand-gallon-a-minute rear-mounted pumps. They carried five hundred gallons of water so you could get a jet to work immediately if required.

These machines were the fastest machines that I ever drove, they could move like bats out of hell, but the trouble was stopping the ruddy things. The braking system was not what it should be and when you wound these machines up they needed a good stopping distance, and the other drawback was the fuel consumption – they were real petrol guzzlers.

Eventually these machines were replaced by Leyland vehicles with midship fitted engines and front-mounted pumps, they were diesel engines and they did not have the zip of the Rolls Dennis.

The escapes, which were made of wood although there were some metal ones, were fifty-foot escapes mounted on wheels, the weight was about three-quarters of a ton, but with a good crew these could be slipped from the appliance, wheeled into position and extended in a very short space of time.

Years later when it was decided to replace these escapes with Merryweather and Lacon ladders, which would reach the same heights, we had a competition at London Road to see which could be got to work quickest, the wheeled escapes won hands down. They were eventually replaced because it was decided and it was a fact that the new ladders could operate in much more confined spaces, but quite honestly I and a good number of other lads thought they were very cumbersome to work with.

Years before when fire brigades were just being formed, it was found that seamen were best suited for the job as they were used to long hours and the not so comfortable accommodation. This meant a lot of brigades were run on naval lines; London Road was commonly known as the flagship.

Saturday morning was the chief officer's rounds of the station, first stop being the canteen where all the cutlery was laid out in circles of two dozen, and the plates stacked in two dozens. He would go round with his entourage and the station clerk would check the items against the total for the previous week against the inventory – the chief officer was an ex-lieutenant commander Royal Navy, and quite an eccentric gentleman he was, but more of that later.

It was not long before I was in action with my new mates, we got a call early one evening to a garage on fire and when we arrived we were informed that an acetylene gas bottle was involved. Whilst endeavouring to get close enough to put a spray jet on the cylinder the damn thing exploded; very fortunately no one was hurt but a couple of the lads were bowled up the street from the blast, they had a few bumps and bruises. The valve group from the cylinder was found embedded in the gable end of a house two hundred yards away, that would have made a nasty hole in anyone unlucky enough to have been in the way of it.

Later that same tour of duty we got a call to an old underground air raid shelter in which a firm had stored bales of waste paper. Two of us were ordered in with a jet and within feet of the entrance we were on our guts hugging the floor, it was that thick with smoke and heat. We lay there directing the jet to where we thought the fire was when I was literally lifted to my feet by Stn O Williams, who said, 'If I can stand up in it so can you.'

We always thought he had asbestos lungs and after this episode we were convinced, but he was always there when you needed him, he was extremely well thought of and in my years of service I never met a better fireman. You could have turned up at a job with forty people hanging out of a building waiting to be rescued but old Bungay never changed, always calm and methodical, he was a man you trusted with your life. If he said go in there in you went knowing Bungay had weighed up all the pros and cons first.

It was a strange thing with firemen who smoked, you could come out of a job coughing your lungs up and spitting out cobs of soot, but the first thing you did when you got a chance was to light a fag up, it always felt good.

Working the City

Whilst London Road was headquarters station, there were four substations on the north side of the city and five stations on the south side which included the busiest station in the brigade called Moss Side. This was about the time that the West Indian immigrants were arriving in Manchester and the Moss Side area was where they put down their roots.

Years before this particular area had been the residential area of a lot of Manchester's merchants so there were lots of big old houses which very quickly got converted into flats and overcrowding was rife.

Worse still was the amount of paraffin heaters you found in these places in the winter months. They obviously felt the cold, so everywhere you looked would be a heater, the fatalities that occurred in the early days through someone kicking a heater over at the top of the stairs or in a bedroom was unbelievable.

One incident that was related to me was of Moss Side's getting a call one Saturday night to a house fire, from which they rescued two children, one unfortunately died. There was no sign of their parents but the police eventually found them in a shabeen (drinking den), and when they were brought to the incident and told of the situation there were no tears from the parents, they just accepted it and went along to hospital to see the other child.

This was not the end of this situation for twelve months after, the brigade were called to the same address again on a

Saturday night and once again they fetched out two children, both of whom died, one was only weeks old, the other being the child that had been rescued twelve months earlier. I will leave it to the reader to imagine what the crews said and thought.

Years later I was involved in an incident in Moss Side's area, again on a Saturday night. We got a call to a house fire and on arrival we found the ground floor well alight and we were informed that there were children in the house. Now as soon as we got into the house we could smell paraffin in the hallway, but two BA men found the two children dead behind a bedroom door at the top of the stairs. Due to the suspicious circumstances the police were called in.

As was usually the case at a fire a crowd had gathered outside and when it became known that two children had died a young women appeared out of the crowd and informed the police that she and a man were responsible for the fire, she was arrested and taken away.

The police eventually arrested a man in Glasgow a few days later and he was also charged, but it was not till the case came to court a few months later that the whole story emerged. The lady who lived in the house had apparently stolen her man, so the young women who was on trial had got a man to set fire to the house, whilst the other woman was out, but unfortunately they had not realised that the children were at home.

The man was given a long sentence and the young woman also went to prison, but the ironic thing about this was that a good number of years later the man was released from a Scottish jail and within three days was arrested and charged with killing a policeman within hours of his release

It was not long before I got involved in part-time work again, our hours having been reduced to a fifty-six-hour week gave us a little more time off. I was approached by a publican in the village were I lived, he asked if I would

Snowcem the outside of his premises. I went along and had a look and realised I would take forever doing it on my own, so I asked my mate Ginge if he would come in on it with me, and he agreed so we set to and started the job. We had explained to the landlord that it would be in our time only when we were on nights or days off. Anyhow we completed the job and got paid, he then asked us if we could decorate the interior of the pub, again a price was agreed on and we set about this job.

It was then that we found ourselves inundated with offers of work in the area, mostly to Snowcem the big posh houses of the Cheshire set. We were working every hour God sent and seeing very little of our families, so we decided to ease off a little as we were going on duty fit for nothing. If we got a working job during the night we were absolutely shattered next day, so we got a little more selective in our part-time and eased up. Now I was going up in the world and I was even able to pay for a holiday in Anglesey.

When my holiday was over I went back on duty and was informed that the staff officer wanted to see me, so off I went and he said that my progress had been monitored and they were satisfied, and it had been decided that my probation period would be terminated.

If I could pay back the superannuation I had received from the Anglian Brigade they would count my previous service, which in turn gave me senior fireman's pay in a further few months' time. This was all too good to be true, so here I was only on the watch a few months and no longer the junior man, this meant I did not get all the mundane tasks all the time, and a few extra bob in the bargain.

I was informed that I would have to requalify for my BA certificate as Manchester would not recognise the one issued by the County, so back on a course I went. This was conducted by the same Sub O who was the physical training instructor. The torture chamber again was in an old air raid shelter at a place called Nell Lane, the sets were one and two-hour sets and after the usual thorough theory course, it was on to the practical side and our instructor did not hold back with the smoke and heat. When you emerged from the chamber on your practical drills you were totally dehydrated and, putting it bluntly, very knackered, but when it was all over we felt equipped to tackle any smoke-logged building, although that assumption was to be proved wrong on a good number of occasions. Anyhow it was all over so back to operational duties I went.

Every two years we had to go on a BA refresher course, and if we thought the original BA course was hard this was purgatory, in fact it was so hard that eventually a doctor from the mines rescue was asked to monitor the course. His comments were that mines rescue BA men, who were the bees knees, were not asked to perform the tasks the firemen were doing on their refresher courses, and this eventually got the courses modified.

We started off this course by going through the maze to find a dummy which was then fetched out. Then, without a break you were given four tasks, the first to move a pile of stone sets (cobble stones), which weighed about twenty-five pounds each, from one side of the chamber to the other side. Then we went on to shovel a pile of wet sand from one side of the chamber to the other, before hauling a fifty-six pound weight which was attached to a pulley up and down for two minutes, followed by stepping up and down on a box with alternate feet for two minutes. Believe me, when you finished you just collapsed. Four men carried out these tasks so that as one task was completed they moved round. This is where the clever bit came in they knew no one would stop whilst their partners were carrying on, as they did not want to be classed as a failure. In this way it was ensured that every man would pull his weight.

On the station when we reported for duty, we were detailed off in turn for various tasks, these were dutymen whose job it was to act as a doorman. We attended to people coming to visit the station for information and to ensure the gates were opened for any appliance that was turning out. Also on night duty you had to go down to the appliance room every hour to check under the machines that there were no leaks from the water tanks carried on the machines and that all gates were secure and also when there was a fire call you had to ensure the return gates to the yard were open. Many has been the time when the return gate bell has been rung by a resident returning in the early hours of the morning after a night out and wishing to park their vehicle on the yard. They were not very popular.

Another duty, which to me was the worst of the lot, was being detailed off as boilerman. In the early days, the heating and hot water was supplied by means of a coke-fired boiler, and the boilerman was responsible for this. On night duty you had to stoke up late at night and put the damper down and early next morning you went down and cleaned out all the clinker and got the fire roaring again. Woe betide the boilerman who let the water system get cold. Fortunately this did not last too long as they installed a oil-fired system.

Another duty was the orderly who was responsible for keeping the mess clean, sugar bowls filled and in general assisted the civilian kitchen staff as required.

Every summer at London Road we had the job of limewashing the basement area of the station. A number of men were detailed off every day to carry out this task. They put on overalls and covered their heads with anything that would keep the damn limewash out of their hair. The wash was applied by means of Turk's head brushes; it was a filthy laborious task, and when the bells went you had to rip off all the protective clothing before you could put on your fire gear.

This went on for a number of years until someone in there wisdom decided that the ceiling and walls would be sprayed with a plastic type compound which could be wiped clean with a damp cloth, no one was sorry to see that task go by the board.

Another annual event was that each appliance would be cleansed underneath by means of paraffin and brushes, the appliance was put over a pit in the workshops and the men would carry out this task, and a filthy task it was. This came to a end when the city bus depot got steam cleaning facilities and the machines were done at the bus depot.

The Real Firemen

Contrary to what is shown on TV programmes and films, firemen do not spend all their time on duty playing snooker and cards. On day shift for example after checking the machines we would have our volleyball, followed by drills, and certain days of the week these went on till lunch time. Then after lunch it was cleaning appliances and equipment and one crew would go out on visits to high-risk premises or go and do routine fire prevention inspections, and these could be a real eye-opener.

A classic example of this was visiting a clothing manufacturer in the Strangeways area of the city one afternoon. Now the Fire Service Act lays down how many people may be employed in a building before certain acts come into force but there were exceptions to these rules and one was that if the employees were relatives of the owner the act need not apply.

We visited this three-floored building owned and run by a Asian family, and the first thing that struck us was the number of people working there. Our boss asked the owner about this and the reply was they are brothers, sisters, aunts and uncles, and they were within the law. But on our way round the premises we saw the fire exit doors were unlocked, which was as it should be, but one of the lads decided to try the door so he pushed the panic bolt but the door would not open. We assumed that there must be rubbish up against the door on the outside so the owner's attention was drawn to this and he explained that he had

had that many break-ins to his premises that he had brick walls built in front of the doors. He was given twenty-four hours to have the walls removed to allow the doors to perform their original function.

Some of the excuses offered really had to be heard to be believed. I have seen holes cut in floors to allow boxes to be passed up or down to floors below. These were not fenced off although the employees knew they were there and walked round them, but I saw on a couple of occasions firemen searching a building in dark smoky conditions actually falling through such holes. Whilst we were taught to move our feet carefully to feel for such things, no one is infallible. Some of these people would complain that we were picking on them due to their race, it was a very difficult situation for the officer in charge to explain it was no such thing.

I was member of a crew that attended a call to a house fire in the early part of the evening, now the first thing the officer in charge asked was whether there was anyone in the building, and if the answer was in the affirmative the officer in charge would send back the message 'Persons Reported' and further back-up appliances would be automatically sent to the incident. But at this particular incident, as we arrived there were three Asians trying to get a sideboard down a hall which obstructed our entrance. The officer asked the usual question but we could get no sense from them as they were all excited and would speak no English to us, all they were interested in was getting the furniture out of the house.

The fire was in a bedroom so when the gentle and polite methods failed we moved them aside and got into the bedroom where a quick blast from a small jet quietened it down and to our horror we found two young children dead in a bed. They had been asphyxiated – I think I can leave the reader to draw their own conclusions of our feelings that evening, it appeared that furniture was more important than human life.

Some of the situations we witnessed took a lot of comprehension but if we let ourselves dwell too much on individual incidents we would have been unable to carry on with our job. I have often been asked whether I was affected by what I had witnessed and I can say in all honesty that the only time I felt any emotion was when small children were involved; adults did not affect me at all and I believe most firemen feel the same.

Years later I recollect getting a call to a house about half past seven on a Christmas Day morning, when we arrived we were informed there were three children and a women in the bedroom. Now the ground floor was well alight when we arrived and the staircase at the end of the hall had been burnt through so entry was made through a front bedroom window. Whilst this was happening a women jumped from the back bedroom window into the back garden, the lads got into the back bedroom and fetched out three children but unfortunately they were all beyond our help. On asking the man of the house, who incidentally was outside the house when we arrived, he told us that they had had a party on Christmas Eve and during the party a cushion on the settee was found to be smouldering, possibly from a cigarette end. They had thrown the cushion into the back garden and carried on with the party till the early hours of the morning.

They had retired to bed and next morning they heard the children get up and go downstairs to open their presents up. They had opened the lounge door to be met with a room full of smoke so they had run back up the stairs to tell their father, who came down and found the settee smouldering. He attempted to pull the settee through the lounge door to get it outside and it promptly got stuck.

He ran out to phone the fire brigade from a nearby call box leaving the door open and, as it was said at the inquest, the settee just burst into flames fed by oxygen from the open door. By this time the children had run into the back bedroom followed by their mother but by this time the heat and smoke must have been tremendous and panic would naturally follow. The lady had jumped through the window as we arrived, but she had been unable to locate the children in the smoke. That was the morning I heard a fireman say that there cannot be such a thing as God otherwise he would not let three innocent children die on his son's birthday. It certainly made you think, but again if you dwelt on these things you would never do your job, although I do remember going home and playing with my children and their new toys and I could not help but think about it.

The fire service is always good for a laugh with a lot of great characters, but also some daft ones. One night one of the lads was working on his motorbike. As he was tightening a bolt up, the spanner slipped and he gashed his arm very deeply on a projection from the exhaust. He came to the dutyman for a dressing to put over it, out of the first aid box, but before doing this he had actually stitched the cut together using a needle and thread. He refused to go to hospital and told the dutyman he was not to tell the boss, he actually cut the thread stitches out eight days later, whilst the cut had healed together it left an almighty scar. This same chap had a party piece of dropping down the fireman's pole head first, he had it timed to perfection, he would drop down and just as you thought he was going to hit the rubber mat with a bang he would stop and get up.

In the March of 1961 my wife announced that we were going to have a further addition to our family. We started to prepare for the addition with my mother-in-law making children's clothes on her sewing machine. She was a very accomplished seamstress, and she would make up a dress or a suit in no time.

With the money from my part-time work I was able to buy a new pram with all the other requirements for a new baby.

Sports and Social

By this time I had acquired a permanent place in the brigade soccer team, and we got some decent trips out to play other brigades throughout the country, but the game we all used to look forward to was against the RN submariners. Every year two submarines would come up the Manchester Ship Canal on a courtesy visit.

Now the chief being an ex-Lt/Commander would meet these subs half way down the canal and go aboard for his pink gins in the wardroom and when they berthed at Manchester he would wait till the ship to shore telephone was connected then phone brigade control and tell them to get hold of someone to organise a soccer match. He did this one Saturday evening and after a lot of phoning round, the city police agreed to let us use their ground on a Sunday morning.

So off we went to play this match, the chief and other senior officers plus the subs' skippers all came to watch. We beat them five–nil and after the game we all adjourned to the police social club. When we walked in the chief was already there and he said, 'Bloody good show, chaps.' Then to the stewardess he said, 'Get twenty-two pints in for the boys,' as he said that he turned to a senior brigade officer and said, 'Pay for this order.' A shocked officer promptly made out a chit for the drinks payable from the fire brigade sports and social club. Then in the afternoon we would visit the boats and have a good time, this was in the days before HM ships were made dry with no grog issue, but we used to go into the chief and petty officers' mess and they would have saved us some neat tots and damn good stuff it was.

We in turn would lay on a party for them in our social club and invite nurses from the local hospital. We had some wild nights and I never recollect any trouble in any shape or form, these matelots were a credit to the service, before they left they used to present us with a crest of their boat, which were all hung in the bar as mementoes of a good time.

Whilst we were on night duty we were allowed to go to the bar on our stand easy time, that is with the exception of the first pump/escape crew who stayed in close proximity to the engine house. This machine was first away to any call we got in the city.

All the men knew the situation as concerned drinking, it was kept to moderation, especially the drivers. A pint would last all night as this privilege was not abused because to do so would put the bar off limits for all on duty personnel. When the bells went there was an almighty rush, you had to run down four flights of steel stairs and across the yard and onto your appliance.

A Birth, a Death

My wife went into hospital to have the baby just after Christmas in 1961 and I had been granted a few days' leave. The night before my leave started I was on nights and we got a call to a house fire at about eight o'clock in the morning. When we arrived a lady was stood outside screaming, 'My baby, my baby.' We managed to get her to tell us where the baby was and she said in the back room in a cot. The ground floor of the house was well alight but I was one of the BA men and we managed to get into the back room and we found the cot and stripped it, but no baby.

We then did a thorough search of the room before moving into the front bedroom, we found a double bed and stripped that but still no child. Then I was on my hands and knees under and around the bed, I felt under a chest of drawers and felt what I thought was a dolly, I picked it up and had a close look with the aid of my lamp and realised it was a baby.

By this time it was a hopeless task to try and resuscitate the child as it had been a long time before we located it. I informed my mate, and I carried the baby out and placed it in the waiting ambulance. When I told the officer where I had found the child, like me he could not understand how the mother had been so adamant that the child was in the back room where we wasted valuable time searching. Anyhow we made up our gear and went back to the station and that day, the 30th December, my second daughter was born and I thought how unfair – a child born and one tiny mite dead on the same day. It was not until we attended the inquest a while later that the full story emerged. The father had got up and lit the fire in the back kitchen, and as was usual he placed a fireguard around the fire and placed on it the baby's nappies to dry which had been washed the night before. He had then gone off to his work, and a spark or the fact that the nappies were too close to the fire had ignited them. The lady in her evidence said that she woke up coughing and realised the house was on fire. As she went across the landing to the back bedroom she remembered their pet mongrel dog brushing past her legs on the landing, she got into the back room where her screams were heard by a neighbour who assisted her from the back window via a short ladder that someone else had brought.

When asked why she had told us that the child was in the back room she said that during the night the baby had been crying and she had got up and put the baby in bed with her husband and herself. When she awoke she dashed into the back room having forgotten she had taken the baby out during the night and she was so panic-stricken when we arrived that she could not remember having moved the baby.

In giving my evidence I was shown a photograph taken by the police photographer of a chest of drawers under which there was a dog lying. I was asked if I had felt or seen the dog, the answer to that was no, my hand must have been inches away from the dog when I found the child. The police surgeon who carried out the post mortem said that in his opinion the dog had grabbed the child from the bed and taken it under the chest of drawers, small marks on the child's body being consistent with the child having been gripped by the dog's teeth. This really made me wonder if the dog really was trying to save the child, in my opinion I am convinced that the dog had tried to take the child to a place of safety.

Demonstrating for a few pounds more in 1971

A special service call
Photograph reproduced with kind permission from G.M.C. Fire Service Museum. ©

Trainee junior firemen

A small factory fire
Photograph reproduced with kind permission from G.M.C. Fire Service Museum. ©

Home Office inspection at London Road

Funeral of ex-city of Manchester Chief Fire Officer
Photograph reproduced with kind permission from G.M.C. Fire Service Museum. ©

Pauldens department store

The twenty-pump fire at Jewsbury and Brown,
Ardwick Green, 21st August 1953
Photograph reproduced with kind permission from G.M.C. Fire Service Museum. ©

On the Move Again

In the spring of 1962 I set off for work one Sunday morning to find that due to electrification of the railway line from Crewe to Manchester the train I normally caught was not running and that we would be bussed down the line to a station five miles farther on. Consequently I arrived for duty half an hour late. I was promptly charged with being absent from my place of duty, I appeared before my divisional officer and got fined ten bob (fifty pence). Then three weeks later exactly the same thing happened and again I was summoned before the DO and after I explained the situation to him he admonished me then told me it was time for me to think about moving closer to my place of work, there was a flat empty at London Road and I should give it serious consideration. It was said with a inference I was not to keen about.

So I said I would discuss it with my wife. When I came out of his office another fireman was waiting to go in to answer a charge the same as mine, but the excuse that he gave was to become a legend in the brigade. When the reason for being late was asked, he stated that during the night it had been extremely windy and had blown in his bedroom window, he had got up and put a blanket over the frame. Next morning when the knocker-up came he never heard him and had overslept. Knocker-ups were still going then, it was usually an old gentleman with a long bamboo cane, on the end was fastened a few wires and he tapped on your window until you acknowledged him, if I remember correctly it cost half a crown a week, three bob if he came Sunday morning as well. Anyhow after listening to his reason for being late the DO dismissed the charge.

When I got home that night I told my wife what had been said and asked her opinion of the situation, after a long chat we decided to move into London Road.

So here we were on the move again, but it was a decision I was never to regret, the flat was on the top balcony next to the hose tower, no matter what they looked like from the outside these flats had large rooms and all mod cons and all the floors were parquet block and highly polished.

The two eldest children did not take long to settle in as there were plenty of other children to play with and they used to sit for hours on the balcony watching the recruits training and within weeks they could repeat some of the orders they heard from the yard, it was great fun for them.

All the families came round to offer help and advice about schools. For example if a man's wife was ill he always came home to a hot meal that one of the neighbours had cooked, and the ladies used to take it in turn to take the children to and from school, it was a village within a city.

When you were on duty you were not allowed in your flat, officially, but everyone went up to collect clean dry underwear if you came back from a job in a filthy state, which happened quite often.

I used to have all my meals brought down to the canteen for me, rather than eat the mess food which I must add was very palatable.

Nineteen sixty-two arrived and with it I took on a new job, that of bar steward. It paid three pounds ten shillings a week plus ullage. This job entailed opening the bar at 7.30 p.m. till 11 p.m., and when I was on night duty my wife did the relief and she got paid fifteen bob a night (seventy five pence). It had its perks though.

When on day duty I was allowed time off to see to the bar, which got me out of many a drill period. This was a job my wife and I did for five years, in two separate spells, and we really had some good times in there.

Every year they had the pensioners' reunion, which was a big day, the station was made spotless and the club room decorated with flowers from the parks department. In the evening they held a social in the gymnasium for them, believe me, thousands of gallons of water flowed on that night as the tales of the past unfolded. We had a pensioner who had actually served on the horsedrawn appliances, he had actually drawn his pension for more years than he had served. All in all they were given a good day out, at the time you do not think of your own retirement but I have been to a good few since those days in my own right as a pensioner, and it is still brilliant to meet your old mates and have a good old chinwag.

At the end of the day we would all be saying the same thing, 'they do not know what it is all about these days', which is a load of rubbish, they still have fires and they still face the problems we had, perhaps more so now with all the different types of chemicals that they can encounter, they still take the same punishment on a fireground, but it would not do to admit that to the youngsters.

It was not too long after taking over the bar that I was nominated for a driving course, so off I went for a two weeks course taken by our old friend the BA instructor, he was clearly a man of many talents.

At that time there was no such thing as a HGV licence, an ordinary licence covered all. One of his favourite tricks was to take you on the steepest hill in Manchester, stop and place a matchbox behind the rear wheel then tell you to do a hill start. Woe betide the man who squashed his matchbox. After two weeks I passed out, and for four weeks I was allowed to drive fire appliances back from fires, then came the big day when my name was read out to drive the second pump/escape.

When the bells went down I was a bundle of nerves. I jumped into the machine and lucky for me it was a city shout so I just followed the first P/E but when we arrived at the incident my ticker was bouncing away. It really had made my adrenaline flow and, even years after, I still got a big kick out of driving a machine through the city to a shout and best of all when it was peak traffic period in the city when you had to force your way through the traffic. You would go through a gap and feel yourself listening for the crack as you clipped something, I was very lucky I got away with it.

Having got my licence opened a new dimension for part-time work. There was always work to be had driving lorries for firms in and around the city. We had a public call box in the reception hall of the station and from 7.30 a.m. till 8.30 a.m. this phone was constantly ringing with firms looking for part-time drivers for delivering clothing to driving furniture vans, the opportunities were endless.

Some firms were better than others but I got fixed up with a firm delivering windscreens and windows for the motor trade. I used to run to Glasgow in the north, to Bristol in the south west and it paid pretty good. The only trouble was if I was away overnight my wife had to do the bar and it finished up with her doing the bar virtually full time, but no one in the brigade seemed to mind as long as it was open and closed on time, and that the beer was kept in good nick.

It was only natural that some of the driving jobs we took on were jobs that no one else wanted, poor pay and in some cases very poor vehicles; remember at this time there was no such thing as the tyre laws or vehicle test certificate. Some of them were in a terrible state, but it gave us a little extra money to supplement our meagre pay packets. I remember taking a furniture van full of tissues to a warehouse in Swindon, there was holes in the floor of the cab which left my feet frozen, then just outside Swindon whilst climbing a hill the lorry just would not climb the hill even in first gear, so I finished up by finding a alternative route into Swindon which the vehicle could negotiate. I well remember it took me hours to get that ruddy lorry home.

Cleaning routines on the station never altered, for example Friday was scrubbers' day when the engine house floor was cleaned, on the Thursday night shift, a man went into the basement and filled up a two-hundred gallon steel tank with water, into this tank he added soft soap and soda and under the tank was a gas ring and with this lit, the mixture was allowed to bubble away all night, the finished product was called sugee, it really was a powerful cleaning agent.

After parade on Friday morning all the appliances were backed into the yard and the engine house would be given a soak by means of a jet and then a line of men armed with deck scrubs would scrub the floor with sugee. The floor was made of small yellow tiles and it used to come up clean enough for you to eat your lunch off. After scrubbing it would be rinsed off with a jet and all excess water would be mopped up until the floor was dry.

Then men were detailed off to wash and polish the appliances and others to clean the engine house poles and brass slides for the doors, there were seven poles in the engine house and to be detailed off for this job was not one of the favourite tasks. You cleaned each pole with Brasso and then gave the pole a good polish. If you were unlucky enough to get a bell whilst doing this job you just hoped that no one came down the officers' mess pole before all the Brasso had been cleaned off because this left white marks on your trouser legs that could not be cleaned off.

Woe betide the lad who was unfortunate enough to land in that situation.

The machines were washed and polished and the tyre walls were polished. This cleaning was in addition to the fact that every time you turned out no matter what time of day or night the machine was always rinsed off on return to the station. To the layman this may have seemed like a load of bull but it was a routine that was accepted without question by the crews.

Saturday morning all the balconies were washed off and it did not matter if it was bucketing down with rain, snowing or whatever. The book said the balconies would be washed every Saturday so they were, then from one o'clock we were on stand easy till going home time.

Saturday afternoon most of the lads who were lucky enough to have cars would give them a wash and clean on the yard. It was very rare that any of these routines varied, to the children on the station it was great fun to wait till you had scrubbed a balcony and then a couple of little bodies would appear with chalk and scrawl all over the floors.

Officially children were not allowed on the yard because of the constant movement of appliances but even so you treated the yard with utmost caution when driving back in from a fire call as they would appear from nowhere, the things they found to amuse themselves with was nobody's business. Sometimes they went a bit too far, like the youngster who got into the milkman's electric milkfloat and drove into the hose tower, or the little devil who got the snooker balls out of the snooker room and stood on the second balcony, dropping them onto the lads' cars, now he was not a popular boy.

One evening on night duty I had gone up to the bar and the bells went. As I was on a back machine I allowed the other crews to go first and when I set off running along the balcony I was whipped off my feet and the next thing I knew was waking up in hospital. What had happened I was to find out later, was early in the evening some of the children, including my son, had tied a piece of rope to the top balcony and lowered it down to the next balcony where they had tied a loop in it to use as a swing. When they had been called in at bedtime they had left this swing in position, and the lads running out of the bar in front of me had brushed the rope to one side. As I ran past I didn't see it and it caught me under the chin swinging me backwards and I must have clouted my head on the balcony floor, which knocked me out and gave me a good case of concussion. I was taken to hospital as a precautionary measure, and when I came out I could not bring myself to admonish the children concerned but it was pointed out how dangerous it was; but what the hell, we were all young once.

Another of the tricks the youngsters liked to do was to wait till a hose was being washed and then run past the washer getting themselves soaked through, it was a great game, especially in the warm weather.

I saw youngsters sit on the balcony yelling out orders to the recruits, they had heard them that many times they knew them off to perfection, but in general the children on the station did not cause too many problems.

One day one of the lads asked me to do him a favour, he was supposed to drive a funeral car for a hire firm in the city and something had cropped up and he could not go so he asked me if I would do it for him. Off I went to pick up this Humber Snipe car, and the address I was sent to was on a council estate outside the city.

I arrived at the house and knocked on the door. A man dressed in a pinstripe morning suit and yellow gloves answered the door and told me to wait in the car as the hearse had not yet arrived. This I did and eventually a hearse with a coffin in the back arrived. The man came out and asked me to help them with the coffin which was extremely light and we took it into the house into the front room and there laid out on a door placed on two trestles was the body of a old gentleman dressed in a old flannelette-type night shirt. The undertaker asked us to help him place the corpse into the coffin, which we did, and after screwing the lid down we put the coffin in the back of the hearse. Neither myself nor the other driver had spoken we were too flabbergasted with all this going on. He then told me to follow the hearse, so we set out to another house on the estate, where there was a group of mourners.

We set off for the crematorium and afterwards took the mourners to a restaurant in the city, when I got back to the hire firm I told the owner of what I had done and he replied that he was an insurance salesman and he did these funerals for his clients on the cheap. When I asked him how he got the corpse to his house, he told me that the agent and his brother-in-law picked it up at night in a van and took it to his house to lay it out, this had been going on for sometime but shortly after that he was found out and all his activities came to an end.

It was amazing the number of firemen who did undertaking in their spare time, it used to be ten bob (fifty pence) a funeral and fifteen bob (seventy-five pence) if you carried the coffin into the church or crematorium. I did quite a few funerals but it was not my favourite part-time job.

One day on the first occasion I had ever done a Catholic funeral, as we carried the coffin into the church the priest sloshed water onto me. I was that shocked I nearly dropped my end of the coffin.

Funerals which are normally solemn occasions can have some funny moments. We did one funeral and the grave was close up to the cemetery wall so when it came to lowering the coffin into the grave it would not go down because of the footings of the wall, we finished up standing the coffin almost upright to slide it in, the mourners were very upset.

The same cars we used for funerals would be in use on Saturdays for weddings.

That year I took my sub officer's exam only to find I had failed on the subject of hydraulics again, but the enthusiasm I had at the beginning was wearing a bit thin as I was too tied up in part-time work to find much time for studying.

It was about this time that the chief officer asked for some volunteers to crew his yacht to Germany where he had apparently hired it to someone. He got his crew and off they went, when they arrived the chief thanked them and they were left to make their own way back to the UK. This was the sort of man he was.

Another of the stories of the chief was that on Saturday nights heads of departments took it in turn to host a party with different themes. One Saturday morning he arrived at the station for his usual rounds but before commencing he told the officer in charge that he wanted two men and the general purpose lorry, they were told to go to a builders' merchant, pick up a load of sand and then take it to his house. The lads had to shovel the sand through a ground floor window where all the carpets had been removed and then spread the sand about. His theme for the evening was a South Sea islands night with wicker tables with pineapples and dishes of nuts on them, but on the Monday two men were detailed off to shovel the sand back on a lorry and take it to another builders' merchants where, it was said, he sold it cheaply. As I said the chief was a likeable but eccentric man, he was apparently a financial genius in running the brigade on a shoestring. The story goes that the brigade engineer asked for a number of pounds for tyres for the appliances for the year the chief promptly cut the figure by half and told him to get on with it, and he bought four second-hand appliances from the County to use as reserve machines; these machines were never off the run.

One of his favourite tricks was to invite people who come to visit his home to see the fire station, and then when they arrived he would have the bells put down for a test turn out and we would finish up on the yard at all hours of the evening doing drills to impress his visitors.

The one to beat them all was when he invited a group of pupils from the famous Gordonstoun school to come and spend two weeks at London Road fire station and ride the appliances to fires. They were not to get involved but just to observe. They came for about four successive years, what the idea was no one had any idea, but a few suggestions were made which would not be too many miles from the truth. As far as the men were concerned they were a pain in the bum, a bunch of spoiled rich brats who were never likely to do a day's manual work in their lives, they could not have cared less, they were there because someone thought it would be a jolly good wheeze to tell their friends about how they had ridden to fires in a large city brigade. I expect half of them are now running our country.

One of the most interesting appliances to ride was the emergency tender. This appliance attended most road traffic accidents and the like, and it attended most make up calls. It carried all the specialised equipment that we were likely to require including BA sets that had a duration of two hours, and all the facilities for servicing BA sets out on the fireground, also it carried heavy lifting gear and it still carried a sling and lifting gear to lift horses out of collapsed roads. This gear dated back years to the days when horse and carts were the order of the day as far as transport was concerned, I never saw it used.

I was on this machine one Friday morning when we got a call in the middle of scrubbers' to attend a fire on board a vessel called the *SS Plainsman*, which was berthed in Manchester docks. This area was in fact Salford's area and we were requested on the make up for more men to wear BA. When we arrived we were informed that the fire was in cotton bales which were not burning openly but smouldering, but on top of the bales had been loaded bags of fish meal. We were detailed off to go into the hold and put the bags of fish meal into slings which in turn were swung onto the dockside. We spent a maximum time of fifteen minutes in the hold before we were relieved as the heat was tremendous. When eventually we got to the cotton bales the same procedure was adopted to get them out, but after about a half hour the operation was suspended because the crane driver and the dockies went on strike for so called dirt money because of the smoke. These people were in the fresh air just removing the bales from the slings and the firemen were opening and damping them down, after negotiations with the management they got a substantial hourly pay rise and we the people down below who were getting a pasting in heat and smoke were on a pittance compared to the dockies' hourly rate. During one of our rest breaks one of the lads mentioned this to a dockie and the answer he got was that is what the union was for, why didn't we do the same? There was no answer to that, he would not have understood.

After it was all over we returned to the station and no one would come near us as the smell of the fish meal was overpowering. All our fire gear had to be sent away for cleaning but the damn stuff seemed to cling to our skin for days after. Those were the sort of jobs you did not want many of, but whilst it was hot it was not the hottest I ever experienced, that was still to come.

In the city we used to get quite a good number of calls to the seedier type of night clubs, and for some reason or other they always seemed to be located in basements. They were hellish to get into because the heat would hit you as you went down the stairs. It turned out that a awful lot of these club fires were arson jobs, and when you extinguished the fire it was nothing unusual to find fruit machines and cigarette machines smashed open and the contents of the same emptied.

The next course I was nominated for was a turntable ladder operator. This was a very interesting course, it was amazing where you could place the head of a one-hundred-foot turntable ladder. In the city with its narrow back streets you had to judge if you had enough room to rotate the ladder as well as for watching for overhead cables and obstructions. We were also taught how to rescue people using the slings and lowering line, all in all I really enjoyed this course and at the end it was another qualification by my name. I was now eligible to drive and operate any appliance in use in Manchester fire brigade.

Not long after I had completed this course a well-known firm of pest control people hired a turntable ladder for a job in the city on a Sunday morning. I was detailed off for this job and I was ordered to cover up the Manchester Fire Brigade logo on the appliance with the aid of masking tape, then off I went with one crew man. When we arrived at our destination I was told what was required of me, they wanted a line of a jelly-like substance applied to the window sills of several large buildings in the city. This substance was to stop starlings and pigeons from roosting on the sills at night, as the droppings on the sills were unacceptable. The birds alighted on the sills onto the jelly and the idea was to make the birds feel unstable. This must have cost the firm a bomb but it was a nice change for me and also good practice as some of the buildings were in the narrow streets of the city.

Whilst I was called upon to operate a turntable ladder for use as water towers I was never called upon to rescue anyone, although it was a common drill to fetch lads off the hose tower and various roofs on the station. Sunday mornings we would go to various areas in the city to practise shots with the TTL in the narrow back streets around some of the biggest stores in the city. My friend Ginge had cause to thank these sessions when after I had retired he was called upon in the seventies to use his skills with a hydraulic platform at a very serious fire at Woolworth's store in the city, the hydraulic platforms began to take the place of the TTLs.

With the children growing up and attending school, even the youngest was going to primary school, my wife decided to go back to work, so she started as a GPO telephonist in the city. After arranging to have the children looked after by a lady on the station when I was on duty, this was the signal for me to ease up on the part-time work. We were able to manage financially so I began to devote more of my spare time to my hobby of fishing, which eventually paid off for me as I was lucky enough to be a member of the team that won the All England fire brigade championship, a first for Manchester.

It was about this time that we started to have our annual holidays, camping in Scotland and needless to say I did an awful lot of fishing up there and made a lot of friends, so much so that when I retired from the service I went to live up there but that is another story.

There was a little job we got called upon to do quite often being residents on the station. The sergeant from the coroner's court would come and ask for two or three of us to sit on the jury on inquests. We did this on a good number of occasions as we got paid seventy-five pence a session and if, for example, the case involved two deaths in a road accident we got one pound fifty. The only cases we were not allowed to sit on was any that the fire service had been involved with, such as road traffic accidents or fires.

Saturday evening was the time of many road accidents involving fatalities, and right outside the fire station was the scene of many a horror story. The very busy junction was not controlled by traffic lights and we could sit in the canteen on a Saturday night and wait to hear the bumps before the bells went down. It was here that I witnessed something I would not have believed if I had not seen it, a mini car hit an articulated lorry at such a angle and such speed that it knocked the front axle from under the lorry, which incidentally was fully laden. The driver got away with a fractured leg and cuts, the driver of the lorry was still in his cab, which was nose down on the floor, and in shock.

Another of our Saturday night sagas used to take place at a pub which was alongside a lock on the canal. The pub was frequented by gays and transvestites, very often we would get a call to pull 'Esther' out of the lock where he/she had been pushed by 'Stella' because he had been trying it on with his boyfriend. We used to pull them out then have to keep them apart till the police arrived. It was the best comedy show you could wish to see, very fortunately the water in the lock was only a couple of foot deep when the lock was empty but it was a drop of about fifteen foot to the water, but what a disaster it was to some of them to have their dresses ruined.

One Saturday evening we got a call to a vehicle that had hit a lamppost, trapping the driver, so off we went and cut the driver out, who was seriously injured. We got him off to hospital and then started to clear up the mess and swill away the petrol. We were ready to go back and just getting aboard the machine when one of the lads thought that he heard a moan. We got off the machine and had a good look around and found a youth in an alleyway about twenty yards from the incident, he was in a serious condition when he was put in the ambulance. On investigation it appeared he had gone through the windscreen and actually rolled into the alleyway out of sight of the main road. If his moan had not been heard he could have lain there all night with possibly fatal results.

What we did find on a lot of road accidents was that you could usually ignore someone who was shouting and screaming and attend to the quiet ones first. If they could scream and shout there was nothing wrong with their breathing.

We have arrived at some road accidents and looking at the mess you would not have given a jot for them being alive but we have taken them out and they have recovered, others we have taken out without a mark on them and they have been dead.

One New Year's Eve we got a call to a smash on a busy road at about 7.30 p.m. When we arrived it was a fifteen-hundredweight van that had hit a small saloon car head on, the driver of the van was staggering about the road until the police put him in a van.

The driver of the car was trapped and obviously in a bad way but worse still was a young lady at the side of him. She had been decapitated and her head lay at the back of the seat. The young man died as we freed him from the wreckage, the man from the van had a minute cut over his eye and we were told he was much the worse for wear with drink. The couple in the car had had nothing to drink they were on their way to a party. The number of road accidents we saw caused by drink driving was amazing and yet I was to become one of those fools, after all I had seen.

A Substation

In 1966 I was transferred to a substation called Upton Street in the Longsight area of Manchester. This was a one pump station which was very busy, the station was very old and was soon to replaced by a new one but it was a happy station with a good variation of risks but mostly residential.

This station's area took in the address of the infamous Hindley and Brady, the house where Hindley lived was a stone's throw from the station.

It was at this station I was to witness my greatest tragedy, one lovely Sunday morning on the 6th June, 1967, about 10.45 a.m. we received instructions from brigade control to go to a location outside our area near Stockport, there were reports of a aeroplane in trouble and losing height.

We were placed on the flight path it was expected to pass over, so we proceeded to the location and saw the plane approaching at a very low altitude. It crashed just outside the town centre about four miles short of Manchester airport, the pilot dropped the plane between two blocks of flats onto some spare ground.

We were instructed to attend the crash site, and when we arrived Stockport's crews were already spraying the wreckage with foam and taking away survivors. It was a British Midland Argonaut plane en route from Majorca with holidaymakers, from the wreckage we took seventy-eight people who were dead from injuries received in the crash. We took out the bodies and laid them out to be taken away and covered them with salvage sheets. Within minutes of the emergency crews arriving, the place was swamped with sightseers and also ice cream vendors. It was a sight I never want to see again, but the ghouls who actually tried to look under the sheets were unbelievable. Some of the lads lost their temper and actually threatened these people. The one thing I must say about this was the brilliant way the pilot dropped the aircraft between the flats as it could easily have been a bigger tragedy than it was.

We spent most of the day there before we returned to the station and believe me, there was very little conversation amongst us for the rest of the shift.

Many years later I was asked my opinion of the decision to award members of the South Yorkshire Constabulary big money payouts for being at the Hillsborough disaster and being so-called traumatised. I thought it was a disgusting decision, it is my belief these police jumped on the American-style gravy train for cash pay outs, to me they were a disgrace to their colleagues. What about firemen and ambulancemen who attended? Did they bleat about being traumatised? As I have stated before, if you were to think about all the things you had seen you would never carry out your job, you must be able to put it all out of your mind.

Lots of incidents spring to mind: Stockport air disaster; in London the Moorgate tube disaster or King's Cross, no I honestly believe they were a disgrace to the police service.

It was whilst serving at this station I saw some of the daftest causes of house fires. One lady, whose bedroom was burnt out, was asked the usual questions about the cause of the fire. The boss asked her if she used an electric blanket, she replied, 'Yes but it could not be that as I only washed it yesterday and it was all right then.'

Or the chap whose living room had been badly damaged, the fire having started in a fusebox. 'The fuse blew last night whilst we were watching TV so having no fuse wire I put a small nail in the fuse holder.' This during the night had glowed that hot it had set fire to the fusebox and surrounding woodwork.

One chap who had his electricity cut off because of non-payment had actually fed a wire from the streetlight outside his house into the fusebox, this in turn overheated the fuses creating a fire.

Another fellow whose gas had been turned off had cut through the incoming pipe and the pipe the other side of the meter and with the aid of a bicycle inner tube and a couple of jubilee clips had bypassed the meter and during the night they had a small gas explosion. The things people do, you get to a stage where you think you cannot see any dafter situations but within a few weeks you see something different. The classic example of some people being naive was the ones who had a fire and then, when they saw the amount of damage done to a bedroom, claimed they had lost a fur coat worth lots of money, when the only fur coat they had ever seen had been on the back of some film star.

Worse still would be the ones who would claim there had been substantial amounts of money in a room before a fire and then when it was out claim that it was missing. This would involve questions by the police and put us in a bad light, but the police were wise to these people.

The biggest scam of course was the insurance claim, for example a small firm might be well alight by the time we got the call and when the fire was out the fire assessors would be there touting for business. The owner would say there were forty shopping bags and two hundred leather wallets in the corner when I left the premises last night and now they are all burnt up. We did not get involved with this sort of thing, we left it to the experts.

It was amazing the things they came up with, particularly with arson cases. For example if petrol had been used to start a fire, when you first entered the building on arriving you could usually smell it even if the fire had a good hold and the severity of charred woodwork was always a clue for the experts to fix how and where a fire had started.

One midweek morning we got a call to a flour mill, and when we arrived there was smoke issuing up through a cavity wall on the top floor of a four-storey mill. It appeared to be a pile of flour dust which was smouldering on a ledge about twenty feet down. This presented quite a problem due to the danger of a dust explosion if the flour was hit with a jet of water or the like. Dust of any kind mixed in the right proportions with oxygen is liable to explode.

After a lot of discussion I volunteered to try and slide down the cavity on a lifeline and if I could reach the ledge I would remove the smouldering flour. Having taken off my boots and fire tunic I made an entry down the cavity, having first tied a lifeline around myself. If the knot failed I could only blame myself. A metal bucket was squashed and also lowered down, and after a struggle I got to the ledge and was able to remove the flour dust which was quite solid. Having removed this into the bucket I assured myself that there was no more remaining flour dust alight, and I called to be hauled up and after quite a struggle I emerged over the top of the ledge. I am assured by my mates that I looked like the little chap on the flour sifting advert on the TV, I was spitting up cobs of dough for an hour after.

This little episode gained me a commendation from the Watch Committee, and one thing stuck in my mind with what one member of the committee said to me, 'We hope your health does not suffer as a result of all the flour dust you inhaled.' At the time of the incident I had never given it a thought, again this was one of the reasons I was known as Slim, I never found out how narrow the cavity was.

One night we came back from a fire to find some nice person had been in the fire station and taken the television set, this was the start of a spate of thefts from the station, when the bells went down the lads would take off their shoes to put on their fire boots en route to the fire. The shoes were left lying on the engine house floor. When these began to disappear there was not a great deal we could do about it because when we turned out the engine house gates were left open and the station unattended, but there was not a lot you could do, only make sure your shoes and any valuables you had went with you.

At one of the substations a tramp used to call around and the lads would always find him a jam buttie or a piece of toast but he got a bit too familiar. One night, when they returned from a shout the sub officer found him lying on his bed, now that was going too far, no more butties for the tramp was the order.

The meths drinkers and winos used to bring us a lot of grief, if you went to a derelict house on fire you had to ensure that there were none of these characters rolled up in a corner and out to the world. It was hard to wake them up.

A classic example of this was one night a machine got called to a local tip to damp it down as the smell was upsetting local residents. Now these tips had been there for years and they were burning in deep pockets. One of the lads fell over a meths drinker who was sat with his legs buried in the tip to his knees. The lad pulled him to one side and to his horror saw that the man's legs were burnt off to the knees yet he was so anaesthetised with meths and other brews that he had never felt a thing. He was taken to hospital and he survived.

Another incident that occurred at a substation is worth recalling. They were called to a house fire and on arrival they were informed that there was no one else in the house, but the lads carried out the normal routine of searching anyhow. One of the lads, on feeling across a bed, felt a body dressed in a nylon nightie, he took hold of the body only to find it was a blow up doll dressed in fancy night attire. He brought it out of the house and confronted the son of the house with it; it was a very red faced youth who admitted it was his and he slept with it. We quite often got a shock with some of the things that people had in their bedrooms and in the event of a fire were left behind in their hurry to get out of the building, and believe me firemen take a bit of shocking.

One Saturday morning I went on duty and was detailed off to drive the appliance, but another lad who had transferred in from another station asked he if he could be allowed to drive to enable to get to know the station area, the officer in charge allowed this, so I sat in the back.

Shortly after, we got a call to a fire, off we went and as soon as I had my fire gear on I leaned over to the front of the appliance to direct the driver. As we passed under a railway bridge we saw a chap on a moped turn from behind an oncoming lorry and literally drive under the front of the appliance. The driver performed miracles in attempting to avoid him but to no avail. When we jumped out of the appliance we found the moped rider behind the appliance, we immediately started to attempt to resuscitate him when we found he was not breathing, and we carried on till an ambulance arrived but with no success.

At the inquest it was established that the rider had been under psychiatric treatment for a long while for a mental disorder, so the verdict was accidental death. But having witnessed this I honestly believe that the rider deliberately drove under the appliance, only for the skill of the driver there could have been more casualties. The appliance came to rest a matter of inches from a solid buttress which supported the railway bridge.

One Friday evening we went out on a stag night for one of the lads and when the pubs closed it was on to a night club, four of us got into a lad's car and off we went. I was wearing an overcoat but on arrival at the club I decided to leave it in the car.

When we came out of the club the car had been broken into and my coat stolen, and that was the end of it or so I thought. About two weeks later we got a call to a house fire in the middle of the morning, off we went and on arrival smoke was issuing from the front door. As one of the lads entered the door a young lady of about sixteen stone in weight and also about eight and a half months pregnant fell on him in the hall. After we had separated them and Frank, who must have been the smallest member of the crew, managed to get his breath back, we went in and found a chip pan on fire in the kitchen.

On my way out I noticed a row of coats on hooks in the hall and behold there was my overcoat that had been stolen. It was quite recognisable as my mine because of a slightly odd button my wife had sewn on it. I asked her where her husband was, her answer was he had been sent down that morning at the local magistrates' court for theft and receiving stolen goods. I did not take the coat back, the price he was paying was worth it.

It was around this time that the city fathers decided that the city centre and surrounding areas would be knocked down to make way for new developments and a big new shopping centre which was to be named the Arndale Centre, a site that was to become a target for the IRA in 1996.

It was on a demolition site that we were called to a serious incident one afternoon. A worker had been sat astride a steel joist in comic book fashion and was burning through the joist with a acetylene torch. When it was burned through it collapsed throwing him off and the other section of joist fell on top of him with some brickwork. With the aid of the work force on the site we lifted the joist clear of the man, and got him into a ambulance. That was the end of it or so we thought, but almost twelve months to the day this rather tall but skinny man walked into London Road fire station with a case containing a dozen bottles of whisky. He gave them to the dutyman with a message, 'These are for the crew who fetched me out of that building in the city when a joist fell on me.'

It turned out that he had spent eleven months in hospital with serious internal injuries, it was a very nice gesture and the bottles were raffled off and the proceeds went to the benevolent fund. When this man had been rescued he weighed about seventeen stones, the day he came into the station he was nine stone, odd pounds, he lost so much weight whilst in hospital.

Whilst all the demolition was taking place we were kept very busy, usually during the night. The contractors would soak the inside of the buildings to be demolished with diesel oil and ignite it as they knocked off work for the day, the idea being that they would burn all the combustible materials and in the morning they would be left with just the shell of a building to demolish, but the fires would get out of control and become a danger to surrounding property, so we would get called out to extinguish the fires.

They demolished the old terraced houses and destroyed the camaraderie that had been present in the terraces and then promptly built blocks of flats which became a haven for all the junkies and thieves. Many law-abiding people had their lives virtually destroyed by this element, so much for modern developments.

The biggest annoyance for us was the number of turn outs we got to people marooned in lifts, that was the ones that had not been vandalised. We had to go to the lift motor room and wind the lift up manually to the floor above where the lift was stuck, the number of old people we have taken out was no one's business, and they would be very distressed.

It was a pity that the people who designed and approved the building of these blocks were not made to reside in them and to see the appalling conditions that good honest people were having to live in. Since I retired from the brigade the blocks have been demolished and terrace-type houses have replaced them and sanity is starting to come back to these areas, which for a long while were no go areas for clean-living people and the police were reluctant to police these areas.

Some of the high-rise office blocks being built also brought their problems with very sophisticated alarm systems being installed and it took months for all the faults to be sorted out satisfactorily. Whenever these alarms activated we had to respond just in case it was a genuine alarm but having responded to the same alarm say five times in five hours got a bit much.

They also built a big new hotel in the city centre that also was a bind. They eventually had to resite all the smoke alarms in the bedrooms because they were too close to the beds and were very sensitive, anyone sitting on the side of the bed having a last cigarette before turning in would set off the alarm, then they would get a shock when someone arrived at the door to check on whether it was a fire or not.

Back to London Road

I spent eighteen months at the substation before I went back to London Road, just in time to be sent on another course, the Police Advanced Driving Course. Someone thought it would improve the quality of brigade drivers, and whilst I am the first to admit it was a brilliant course, I found it difficult to try to drive a fire appliance as you would a police car. There was a slight difference in weight plus some of the appliances were not yet power steered. Now to drive an appliance through the city at peak traffic periods was altogether different than driving a car, but none the less it was a course I very much enjoyed and it certainly improved my driving of my own vehicles over the years.

The police instructors who taught us were fantastic drivers, they would give you a running commentary on what they were doing and why they were doing it. At the end of the course we had to do the same thing, but it did not come as easily as it did for the instructors. The skid pan was another magical day, the things you saw and did was great, it was a super course.

One Saturday night we got a call to a city centre hotel, one of the rather better class of hotels. Now we used to get quite a few false alarms to this hotel when the drunken idiots were active on Saturday nights, so when we got this particular call it was, 'Here we go again.'

It only took a matter of seconds to reach this hotel from the station and you would barely have time to get your fire gear on before we were on the doorstep. This night however as we turned the corner one of the lads saw it coming out of the ground floor windows and so it was, so much for a false alarm. It was a ground floor bar that was well alight and the upper floors were rapidly becoming smokelogged. We were informed that most rooms were occupied, so evacuation of the residents became a priority, whilst a crew fought the fire we were told to put on BA sets and evacuate every room; we had been given master keys by the management so off we went. Now the stories that did the rounds after that fire were every fireman's dream. The hotel was used by aircrews flying into Manchester, we knocked on doors and if there was no answer we let ourselves in. If the reader can visualise being in bed and someone in a BA set walking into your room and saying could you please slip a robe on and come with me to the fire escape, it must have given the residents a shock. These air stewardesses were magic, they were getting out of beds and wearing very little, put on their uniform Macs and with brilliant aplomb saying, 'Okay, we are ready', not a sign of panic, they were brilliant.

The last room I evacuated gave me a laugh after it was all over. I entered the room and there was a rather elderly gentleman in a double bed with a rather attractive very young lady, the man put on his trousers and off we went. I got them to the fire escape and the man said he had left his teeth in a pot on the bedside cabinet so I went back to get them and when I handed them to him outside he put his hand in his back trouser pocket and gave me a five-pound note and said thanks. It was not long before the fire was out and the hotel ventilated so the residents were able to go back to their rooms, but the way the air stewardesses conducted themselves was absolutely brilliant. Their training had really came to the fore as regarding remaining cool and calm in an emergency. I believe most women would have panicked and tried to cover themselves up before doing anything. The talk was of beautiful girls for a few shifts after that.

Another incident that was funny after it was all over, but serious at the time, was one Sunday morning about half past seven, we got a call for a house fire in a substation's area. That station's appliance was already out so that we were the first attendance, and as we turned the corner into this rather long street we saw a woman sat on a bedroom window sill and a little man stood on the pavement with his arms outstretched imploring her to jump. She damaged her ankle but the poor devil who had been imploring her to jump suffered two broken legs. If she had waited a matter of seconds we would have taken her off the sill by ladder, but when there is smoke about people do not stop to think.

The family that lived in the next flat to me gave us all a good laugh, but to him it was an embarrassment. He had spent a couple of days decorating his kitchen and when he finished he decided to make a pan of chips so he prepared everything and put the pan on and then decided to have a bath whilst the chips were cooking, but unknown to him his wife went out and left the pan on. The next thing he knew was four firemen entering his flat to deal with a chip pan on fire. His kitchen needed decorating again after the fire was out, and needless to say his wife and he were not on speaking terms for the next few days, not because of the mess in the kitchen but because the brigade had turned out to his flat and his mates were taking the mickey out of him,

At one period of time people were covering the ceilings of their houses with polystyrene tiles, they stuck them on and emulsioned them. Whilst they looked okay they were a menace in the event of chip pan fires and the like, the fire would ignite the tiles and little droplets of ignited polystyrene would fall on the carpets and furniture and so spread the fire.

The other thing about chip pan fires and the like was the number of people who suffered scalds and burns from the fat. The pan would be on fire and people would open the back door and grab hold of the pan to carry it out and the wind would blow the flames onto their hands or the handle would be that hot that they would drop the pan spilling the fat usually all over their feet, which ended up with very bad scalding. Worse still were the people who panicked and threw water on the chip pan, the consequences of this were catastrophic.

It was in the late sixties that the brigade lost two of our colleagues in tragic circumstances. The first was a station officer from a substation who was on his last tour of duty prior to retiring, they were called to a make up call out of their area and a roof collapsed burying him up to his shoulders in burning debris. The crew managed to get him out but he died in hospital some three weeks later from septicaemia which had developed through the burns he had received.

A few months later the crew from another substation responded to a make up in another brigade's area. This was to a cotton mill, where the fireman and a sub officer were trying to gain access to an upper floor of the mill via an external fire escape, both were wearing BA sets. One of the men had just got through the door when the floor collapsed, the man inside was thrown down to the floor below and buried in rubble and the lad still on the escape was thrown off and he received severe injuries. These incidents left a big cloud over the brigade for quite a while.

As was usual after a tragedy the brigade always organised a concert, the proceeds going to the dependants. We in Manchester were very lucky that we had a gentleman by the name of Bernard Manning who put his club at the disposal of the brigade and he supplied the artists for the evening's entertainment. He is a truly admired for his kindness and benevolence throughout the Manchester fire brigade.

People used to ask me if I ever felt frightened when I was at a fire, the answer to that is yes. Anyone who has never been afraid at a fire is either an liar or a idiot. It is very difficult to explain what it was like going into a heavily smokelogged basement for example, not being able to see a foot beyond your face, and the noises that you can hear of, say, a floor above collapsing, you could hear air being drawn into a fire, and you could feel the draughts this created. Yes, I was scared on numerous occasions, but you learned to live with these situations and the more experienced you became the easier it was for you to pick up danger signs. However there was always the odd one that would come along and claim the life of one of our colleagues.

One that comes to mind happened in Stockport where a Sub O had just made an entry to a building via a ladder into a window, when without any warning a flashover took place and claimed his life. Whenever you saw very thick black heavy smoke it was usually the sign that there was a rapid build-up of heat and that a flashover was likely. I have been on fires where a fireball has rolled right over the top of us when a door as been opened, so yes I have had to change my underpants on return to the station on more than one occasion.

We used to get a lot of calls classed as special service calls, these could range from road traffic accidents to cats trapped up trees. Some of these could be of a humorous nature apart from the serious ones. For example we got a call for a valuable racing pigeon trapped on a roof, and when we arrived one of the older members threw a stone at the roof near the pigeon and off it flew; it was just tired and had landed for a rest.

Friday nights we would get the stag night pranksters, some poor devil would have been chained to a lamppost by his mates and they would debag him and leave him there. We would get a call and off we went to release the poor devil. One which could have had serious results was we had a lad come into the station late at night and his mates had put a rather large padlock around his testicles which had swollen up and he really was in pain. One of the crew got the bolt croppers off the machine to cut the padlock off, well the look on the poor lad's face when he was approached by the fireman with these things had to be seen to be believed. I think he thought he was going to be castrated or something like that but he went a funny shade of white.

Children with heads trapped in railings was another common call out, we found that if you turned the child upside down we could extricate them in some instances, other than that it was cut the rails.

Another situation we found ourselves facing one night was, we got a call for a person trapped in a house but they did not give any specific way except it was not a fire. So along we went to this house to be met by an extremely embarrassed youth who took us in the back room and took his trousers down. He was trapped all right, he had inserted his penis into a piece of copper tubing and got it stuck. He wanted us to get it out for him, but it was not a straightforward operation so the boss called for a ambulance. The youth was transported to the local hospital where under the direction of a doctor who had first given him an injection we cut off the tubing a little at a time with the aid of the ring cutter! I bet it was a long time before that lad tried anything out of the ordinary again.

On the north side of the city was an area very prone to flooding if we got any heavy rains and we got calls to pump out basements and the like which got flooded.

We got one of these calls in the early hours of the morning so along four of us went in the salvage tender and with the aid of a small pump started to empty this flooded basement. After about an hour the boss told one of the lads to see if he could get someone to brew up for us. Now firemen are notorious for tea drinking so at two o'clock in the morning this lad goes of on the scrounge for a brew. He saw a light on in a downstairs window of a nearby house so he knocked on the door and politely asked the young lady if she could oblige him with four cups of tea which she very generously did. After we had drunk the tea the lad took the cups back but he was away for over half an hour before he came back with a rare old story. The women had told him she had always had a yen to make love to a fireman so he had obliged the lady but she would not let him take his fire gear off, now how could the boss rebuke someone who came back with a story like that.

As I have already mentioned, people marooned in lifts was a regular call, but one day around lunch time we got a shout to someone trapped in a lift. When we arrived we found a young boy with his head trapped between the lift cage and the wall of the lift well, it was a case of cutting off the power and starting to dismantle the lift to free him. He was in a bad way but surprisingly conscious, and he kept saying, 'Please help me, Mr Firemen.' Now on the crew we had a big strapping Irish lad who was later to become chief of an Irish brigade. This lad actually bent two-inch angle iron brackets with brute strength to help to free this boy. We eventually got him free and away to hospital where unfortunately he died of his injuries. It transpired at the inquest that the boy and some other youths had been larking about inside the lift during their lunch break and he had got on top of the lift through the flap inside the lift roof to hide from his mates, and he had been looking over the edge of the lift when someone pressed the lift button for an upper floor. When it moved, his head was trapped but before the lift was stopped the damage had been done. The fire service certainly is not the job for anyone who is the least bit squeamish.

Nineteen sixty-eight saw me getting involved with part-time work again, my elder brother left the Royal Navy after twelve years' service and he came to see me one Saturday evening. He asked if I was interested in going into business with him, he wanted to buy a tipper lorry and go into the haulage game, and he convinced me that it would give me a good return for a half share.

I obtained a bank loan and we purchased a brand new six-wheeled lorry and we obtained a contract with a local firm to run stone from the quarries at Buxton to Manchester airport, where they were building an extension to the runway. I took my two weeks' summer leave to show him how to drive the vehicle as he had only driven a car before, and the idea being I would drive the lorry on my days off and him the rest of the time. This was before the time of tachographs came into being so we were driving all hours of day and night. This went on for six months with most of my income going to the bank to pay off the loan and precious little going into to my hand. One day during the winter I decided to have a day off as I had been working non-stop for months. On this particular day I passed by the area where my brother lived and saw the lorry parked up outside a pub. I went in and there he was drinking so I asked him why he was not working. He answered that the roads to Buxton were blocked with snow, which I knew to be a lie as I had seen other tippers coming down the A6 road that morning. This situation happened on a few more occasions and so I decided to pull out of the agreement, he was not very happy about it but I had made my mind up, and the relationship with my brother finished over this matter. He eventually sold the lorry and the last news I had of him he was running a hardware store.

After that little episode I was inundated with offers from other owner-drivers to drive their vehicles whilst they had days off or went on holiday I made more money that way than I did driving for myself, but again I decided once in a while was okay but not every hour I was off duty, another hard lesson had been learned.

I had a further addition to our family but this one came in the shape of a ready-made one. My eldest daughter came home from school one day and said her best friend had not been to school because her mummy had died. Now Carol used to come and spend time at our flat on the school holidays so we knew her quite well. Carol and her mummy had lived together with a rather elderly uncle not far from the station, so I went to see how Carol was and found that she had been taken into care.

I contacted the authorities and asked if she could be allowed to stay with us, they gave permission for us to foster the child who incidentally was eleven and a half years old.

After a few months we asked Carol if she would like us to adopt her legally and she answered in the affirmative. Now the red tape that we went through to eventually achieve this was in my opinion ridiculous, but thinking back on it the authorities have to be so careful, but eventually everything was settled and Carol adopted our surname. She settled in with the rest of the family as if she had known no other, she was a very bright and intelligent child who was to become head girl of the school she attended, she was also a brilliant swimmer and won the junior swimming trophy outright at the brigade swimming gala after winning it three years in succession. She went on to complete a teacher training course at college.

Now with two twelve-year-old daughters and a ten-year-old son plus the youngest girl of eight our flat became a hive of activity with something always going on, the boy learning to play the trumpet, one daughter playing the clarinet and violin and the other girl playing the recorder and the youngest joining in when she was allowed. It really was not a house you could meditate in, but they were all reasonably well behaved.

The day came when one of the girls asked if they could have a piano, and I agreed to look around for a second-hand one. I heard that a fire station in Cheshire had a piano in their social club they did not want, and on inquiring I was told I could have it for nothing if I collected it. I hired a van and off I went one evening to collect it. When I arrived I found to my consternation that it was a baby grand piano but I decided that we had room for it in the girls' big bedroom.

The lads on the station said they would help me with it into the van. Now we had to come down two flights of stairs to the exit and halfway down the second flight the bells went and I was left sitting with my back against the piano waiting for them to return which after a short while they did. The piano was loaded on the van and off I went to London Road.

I now had five flights of steps to contend with to get to my flat. After a quick trip to the training school and half a dozen recruits were rounded up to assist, the stairs were negotiated and the piano put in position. There were lots of threats by me to the girls what would happen to them if this piano was not used, but it was, and one of the girls became a member of the Northern Youth Orchestra. It was nothing unusual to come off duty and find half the school band rehearsing in the flat.

This piano eventually went off to Romania, the skipper of a ship in Manchester docks bought it via a friend who knew me. I had mentioned selling it and buying a smaller one, so six burly seaman arrived on a Wednesday evening with a set of sheer legs on the back of a lorry, the driver having been hired by the skipper with his lorry from drivers waiting at the docks. Within minutes they had it out of the flat over the balcony and onto the lorry, that piano had a chequered career.

The brigade purchased a hydraulic platform, so on another course I went to learn to operate this, it was not long before I was called upon to use this in anger.

We received a call one winter's evening that a man was on a roof at a psychiatric hospital and we were asked to take him off. When we arrived we found that to get to this incident I had to get the appliance under a stone archway which was very low, so with a man on top of the appliance telling me how much room I had, I approached the archway at a snail's pace. I crept the appliance through and in the process scratched a line off the paintwork on the top boom, but once through we could see this patient clinging to a chimney stack about fifty foot up. After getting the appliance positioned, a male nurse and two policemen got in the cage and off we went. I very gently approached the patient who was shouting up at the moon, 'I will get you.' We managed to grab him and the police put handcuffs on him to restrain him. It was not uncommon apparently for this patient to shout at the moon but on this occasion he had shinned up a drainpipe onto the roof, he looked about sixty years old but he was agile. The following morning the brigade engineer was not very happy about my scratching the new appliance but lucky for me the duty officer explained the situation to him and he calmed down.

Once again I sat my exam and once again I failed but this time not on hydraulics but fire prevention, still I applied for promotion whenever vacancies came up but I never even got interviews but what the hell, I still had a job I was extremely happy with.

I continued to play soccer for the brigade on a regular basis, but I had a period of time when I caught a lot of injuries, the first was a broken cheekbone occurred when a forward headed my face instead of the ball, which resulted in a smashed cheekbone and I finished up having plastic surgery.

That was followed by a broken nose, again being headed in the face, but the thing that I remember most about this incident was the way in which the casualty doctor at the hospital put the nose to rights. Whilst I lay on a trolley in the casualty room he put a pair of swabs on sticks up my nostrils and then said take a deep breath, he then proceeded to push these swabs right up my nose and I actually heard and felt the nasal bones go back into position. Talk about tears in your eyes, that doctor was not on my list for a nice Christmas card.

Another incident which occurred was that the brigade team played Bristol in Bristol. We left on a Monday to play the game on Tuesday, and after the game we retired to the social club where a meal and entertainment had been laid on. The consequence is we stayed another night in Bristol. On arrival home on the Wednesday, Ginge and I went up to the flat and found my wife preparing a meal for the children, she asked me where the hell had I been as I should have been home last night, so jokingly I said, 'Sorry, we had to play extra time.' She did not appreciate the joke at all, she happened to be cutting bread at the time and without any further ado she threw the bread knife towards me. It actually stuck in the door frame at the side of my head, this was the signal for Ginge to take off on a three-minute mile. I eventually calmed her down and explained the situation to her, a simple phone call from Bristol would have avoided all the hassle, another lesson learned.

One of my fishing pals was a senior officer in the brigade and one day he asked if I fancied going up to Scotland for three days' fishing on the river Tweed. After getting the go ahead from my wife off we went with another fireman, we stayed in a pub in a tiny village, and this was an education, after a good day's fishing we went back and had a good meal at the pub and then got down to a drinking session with the locals. At eleven o'clock the landlord cleared the pub and said he was going up to bed, he said if we wanted anymore to drink, help yourselves and put the money in a drawer which served as a till. We had another couple of rounds then slid off to bed. It was not a bad sort of pub to stay at, and we stayed there a few times after that.

Whilst we only fished for coarse fish in the river we did get trout and I never went back home without a ten or twelve-pound salmon. These came by courtesy of the commercial net fishermen on the river, whom I had got to know whilst on my camping holidays with the family.

Whilst on one of these trips I asked the senior officer why I never got a interview for promotion, and he answered that I had too many qualifications, so there it was, but what the hell I was happy enough as I was.

When we got back home from that trip I went on duty on a Friday morning and we got a call to a old warehouse in the city. This building was a multiple occupancy, when we arrived at the scene we found the building to be in a very heavily congested area of the city with very narrow streets and cars parked nose to tail. Appliances had to be parked quite a distance away from the incident which was heavily smokelogged, on the ground floor and basement. The fire was in the basement which was being used by an upholstery firm, the upper floors were quickly evacuated and BA crews went in to fight the fire which looked worse than it was but it was giving out plenty of thick smoke. We were informed that an employee had not been accounted for from the basement firm, so extra BA men were put in to try to locate this man but it was a good half hour or so before he was found. He was obviously dead but it was the situation in which he was found which made it unusual, he was located at the far end of the basement in a corner with his head down a drain. He had obviously thought that he would get fresh air from the drain which he must have found whilst crawling about trying to find his way out.

Again this showed what people do when confronted with fire and heavy smoke, and again this fire was attributed to someone smoking and carelessly discarding their cigarette end or a match which in turn had ignited the upholstery materials causing them to smoulder and give off lots of smoke before bursting into flame. When it was all over and we were making our equipment up we encountered a lot of irate motorists who had returned to their cars to find lengths of hose over the bonnets, where it had been necessary to get hoses to the fire in a very congested area.

The following morning we got another nasty incident, the call was for a man trapped on a lorry. When we arrived we found a young man trapped under a heavy steel bed plate from a machine. They had been dismantling this machine on the third floor of an engineering works and were lowering it in slings to the lorry in the yard below when it slipped from the slings and fell onto the driver. We had to jack up the plate until we could slide the slings back under and then lift it clear of the driver, but it was a case of wrap up what was left in a salvage sheet and clear away the mess. It turned out that this driver had only started with the haulage firm that morning, he had started on a Saturday morning to help the firm out, so there it was again when that gentleman up above says it's time to go there is nothing you can do about it.

But it was not all doom and gloom, one morning we got called to a chimney fire in one of the very few domestic dwellings in the city centre. The police had called us out because this chimney was belching thick smoke all over one of the main roads into the city and drivers were having to slow down. Anyhow we arrived and knocked on the door and it was answered by a young lady in a dressing gown, she was surprised as she had not sent for us, but we explained the situation to her and in we went. She was fluttering about and saying she could not afford to pay for the fire brigade; it is amazing how many people thought they had to pay for our services. She went on that much that one of the older members of the crew said to her, 'It's all right love, you can pay us in kind.' Well it quietened her down but then a few moments later she said, 'All right but you will have to come back later.'

Well it turned out that the Sub O in charge that day was a very ardent Methodist churchman, we thought that he was going to have a fit, and as we were coming out of the house the same crewman said to the girl, 'I will be round about ten thirty', to which she replied, 'Okay.' When we got back on the machine the sub blew up and told us that he would put anyone returning to the house on a charge. That was the signal for the mickey-taking to begin, for the next few tours of duty whenever the sub was within earshot someone would say that they had seen a colleague coming out of her house and the sub would start to react until we came clean and told him no one had taken her up on her offer; but these were the light-hearted moments of the job that gave us all a good laugh.

It was around this time my stubbornness nearly got me into hot water. We had a second station officer posted to our watch who, to put it mildly, was considered by all to be something of a prat, full of his own importance. One evening we turned out to a hotel in the city which for weeks we had been plagued with false alarms on the detection system. I was driving the appliance this Stn O was in charge of. En route to the incident he told me to turn down a one-way street to reach the back of this hotel, I refused point blank to carry out his instructions as this was a busy main road in the city centre, and this call was to what we all believed to be a false alarm. When I refused to do his bidding he got very upset and started to poke me in the rib ordering me to do it or else be put on a charge.

Whilst I could handle the verbal abuse I was not going to allow him to interfere with me whilst I was driving, so I promptly told him to stop poking me and I carried on to the entrance of the hotel where on investigation it turned out to be a false alarm. On the way back to the station he told me to go back the way he ordered, I replied I would go back any way he wanted provided he did not interfere with me whilst I was driving and I would not go down one-way streets to make him happy. By this time we were right in the middle of the city and about quarter of a mile from the station, when he ordered me to turn down a side street. I did so and I stopped the appliance got out and told him he could drive the appliance himself, and off I went to walk back to the station. After about one hundred yards I thought better of it and walked back and before he could say anything I told him I would drive it back but on return to the station I would be make a formal complaint to my union rep about his behaviour and that I would call the crew to testify as to his actions.

We got back to the station and I informed the union rep and the crew agreed to act as witnesses if required. I fully expected to be called to the office but was not. A week elapsed before we went on night duty again and he called me into the office to talk to me about the incident. I said I wanted a union rep in the office with us but he said there would be no need for that. The outcome was I went into the office, he told me to listen to what he had to say without interrupting and then I could speak. He then asked if I had family problems or something because I appeared uptight. I let him ramble on about how wrong I was on the night in question to disobey his orders, he was the officer in charge and I should do as he said. After four or five minutes he had finished and told me to speak, allowing me to forget the rank difference, so at that I told him that in no circumstances would I ever except him or anyone else interfering with me whilst I was driving. I also pointed out to him that the only time I could make access into a one-way street the wrong way was to reach a fire in that street. Whilst that vehicle was on the road it was under my control not his, and I finished by saying that I knew I was in the wrong by leaving the appliance as I did but I stood by what I had done and would take the consequences.

He then dismissed me from the office and I never heard another thing about it, but strangely he was posted to the fire prevention department soon after and it was not long before he transferred to another brigade. A long while later I learned that he was trying to prefer a charge against me but a senior officer had told him to forget it as it would not hold up, but once again I had almost dropped myself in it by my rash actions.

Equipment was always being updated and we took delivery of compressed air BA sets to replace our existing sets. After a day's conversion course we all agreed what a vast improvement they were on the oxygen sets, no more nose clips and mouthpieces but a full face mask which gave you air via a demand valve and you had a cool air flow round your face all the time and the difference in weight was magic. They were so much lighter and quick and easy to service after use. Also it allowed operators to talk to one another, something you could not do whilst using the old type mouthpieces.

London fire service lost two men whilst wearing BA at a underground fire at Smithfield market; this led to a lot of changes in BA procedure, guidelines were issued so when entering a building you clipped this to the entry point and as you advanced into the building the line paid out from a pouch attached to your belt. A series of knots with tassels on the line allowed you to find your way out of a building, there were big knots and small knots if you felt the big knot first you knew you were following the line in, the small knots being the first you came across when following the line out of a building.

In the past the control of BA men entering a building had been rather a hit and miss affair, now control procedures were tightened up, you had a tally taken off you when you entered and a time of when you were due out was written on the tally, and there were always reserve BA men standing by. In the event of someone not being out on time, these men came 'm and found you and fetched you out. We also got issued with an alarm system called a DSU. In the event of you getting trouble you activated this alarm and the rescue teams could hear this alarm quite clearly; in the past the only way you communicated with your partner was by clapping your hands or by touch. It may appear difficult to think you could lose all sense of direction in a bedroom that was smokelogged but believe me it was easily done and in the event of say a large basement it was so easy to become lost and then run out of air, so all these new ideas were a godsend to us.

The new sets saved brigades lots of money with the simplicity of servicing and recharging the cylinders with compressed air and they could be done in minutes on the fireground.

One morning we came on duty to be told by the night crew of a terrible incident they had attended. In the early hours of the morning, control received a call to a house fire, but the caller did not give an address but dropped the phone leaving the line open; the girl in control could hear children screaming and a man shouting for the children. The control room girl got the GPO to trace the call and in the meantime put the bells down at all the stations so that as soon as the call was traced she could send the appropriate station. On getting the trace she sent the nearest appliance and a back-up appliance from London Road. On arrival it was found to be a newsagent's shop with a flat above and the shop was well alight and being near to Bonfire Night the shop had a large stock of fireworks in stock, which did not make things any better. The man and the woman were rescued but sad to say both children perished. Now it was policy of Manchester fire brigade to tape all incoming fire calls and this particular section of tape was played back to all of us. The brilliant way in which the young lady in control handled this call was nothing short of a miracle, she could hear the screaming all the time which must have been unnerving for her. On the tape, after the GPO had traced the call, the GPO operator asked her if she wanted them to leave the line open but unsurprisingly she asked for it to be closed as the brigade was on their way and there was no more she could do.

The ladies in control were a very efficient lot, most of them had been in the job for years and they knew the topography of the city like no one's business. They knew as soon as they had the address of an incident, one of them would know in whose station area it was and consequently they would be putting the bells down in that area before the call was completed. They had the wonderful knack of pulling information out of a caller and at the same time calming the caller down, these ladies were the unsung heroines of the fire service. There was one unusual thing about these ladies which no one seemed to understand and that was, why were so many of them spinsters? Perhaps it was because the job entailed so much shiftwork, but even so they were lovely ladies to work with.

The mobilising system from control was brilliant, and when a message was sent back to control it was acted upon straight away with no queries, different from what was yet to come when the Greater Manchester Brigade came into being.

Duty Driver

One of the duty drivers on our watch retired and I was asked if I was interested in the position. I accepted the job, which entailed driving the duty officer to fires not just in London Road's area but throughout the brigade area. I was also responsible for keeping the wireless car clean along with the officer's gear.

The biggest responsibility was knowing your topography, if you were not sure of the address to which you were proceeding you had to tell the officer who would look it up in the *Geographia* and direct you, but it was not very often we got caught out.

One tour of duty you would do number one and then followed by number two the next tour. Number two officer covered if number one was out and an incident occurred where a senior officer's attendance was required. This position exempted you from drills and all the other station routines, we were virtually our own bosses.

It also kept you very busy as you attended most of the calls in the brigade, we had our own bedroom with a telephone and the girls would ring and give you a landmark near the address, it was usually a church or more often than not a pub off a main road.

We got to know all the gossip in the brigade first hand, who was getting promoted and everything else.

Whilst the Land Rovers we used were quite light on the steering we found them very nippy in the city. They could be a bit tricky when you were bobbing along on wet roads but all in all they were ideal for the job.

We carried a thirty-five millimetre cine camera on the first vehicle, the idea being that the duty driver took film at any unusual incidents. I only ever used it once, that was to film a fire at a large timber yard where the fire was literally jumping from one pile of timber to another due to radiated heat, a pile of timber yards from the fire would just explode into flames, it was quite spectacular.

It was whilst I was doing this job of duty driver I saw what I still believe to be the most unfair award of a gallantry medal to a fireman. Late one afternoon we went to an incident on a motorway site where a tipper lorry had slid off the road into a water-filled hole. The driver's feet were held by a vacuum in sand and mud, and the lorry was slowly sinking into the mud. The officer in charge of the first appliance to arrive had requested the emergency tender to attend, but in the meantime he and his crew had got a steel hawser onto a bulldozer to stabilise the lorry and were working up to their necks in water to try and release the driver's feet from the mud. When the ET arrived a fireman put on a BA set, ducked his head under the water and dug the mud away from the driver's feet thus enabling him to be pulled out. The man with the BA set got the Queen's Award for Gallantry whilst the lads who had done all the graft in the initial stages got nothing.

I had seen something similar happen a few years before when one of the lads had snatched a would-be suicide from a dome on a high building in the city, and the officer in charge got a medal. In my opinion medals should not be given for doing the job you elected to do.

People have often asked me what makes a good fireman, well for what they are worth they are:

Fitness – You are required to be fit because of some of the demands asked of you.

Disciplined – He must be prepared to carry out orders especially on the fireground.

Compassion – There are times when you need to understand people's feelings when, for example, they have lost their relatives or belongings in a fire – even their pets, some people can be heartbroken over the loss of a pet.

Loyalty – You are working with the same men all the time, and they must be able to depend on you when needed.

Stubbornness – There are times when you have to make yourself go on no matter what especially in rescue situations when the going can be very tough.

Initiative – The text books cannot cover every aspect of the job, so you must be able to use your initiative.

Common sense – It is no use diving into a situation without thinking, because you can put your mates in jeopardy having to come and get you out.

Love the job – That is self-explanatory.

As duty driver I helped out in the control unit at large incidents, helping to list all the appliances attending and from which stations they came from. On odd occasions when we had very large fires, appliances would come from other brigades to assist, these were the ones always sent back as soon as possible to their own brigades. I did this duty for two years before falling foul of the drink driving law.

It was about this time a new deputy chief was appointed and he was one of the few senior officers who was appointed from an outside brigade. One evening I was number two duty driver when I was told by control to stand by to go with the deputy to an incident on the north side of the city, where some radioactive isotopes used in specialised tracing of cracks in pipes had been lost by the contractor. I was to show the new deputy the way to this incident. After a couple of hours of searching waste land using a type of Geiger counter it was found that a senior member of the company had taken these things home in his car for safe keeping.

It was about three in the morning when after showing the deputy the quickest way to his home he dropped me half a mile from the station and left me to walk back to the station. This did not go down too well with me. This man was to become known as the Smiling Assassin, he had a fixed smile on his face all the time he was speaking to you, then he would gave you a proper rollicking for some misdemeanour or other; and the strange thing about it all was he was the only Manchester senior officer to get a senior officer's position in the reorganised set-up that was to come in 1974.

It started off as a normal week but one in which everything that could go wrong did so. On the Monday I went fishing, and on my return I could not get my vehicle on the station yard due to a function being held in our club. So I parked my vehicle on the car park opposite the station intending to bring it in later. When I went to fetch it I found it had been broken into and all my fishing tackle stolen.

On Tuesday I parked my vehicle in a side street whilst I went to my flat to collect my cheque book and documents for road taxing my car, when I came down I found a traffic warden booking me for parking and also she had called the police because my tax disc was one day out of date. I was told I would be reported even though I showed them the completed form and insurance documents that I had in my hand and that I was on my way to retax the vehicle.

Thursday, one of the lads asked me to drive his father's car from a garage where it had been for repairs and his father was ill. The idea being he would take me in his car to the garage and I would drive his father's car back to the house. Great, no problem, except that on the way back I went through a speed trap at forty-two miles per hour in a thirty-miles-an-hour zone so I was done for speeding, it was turning out to be a great week.

On the Friday evening I went out with a couple of mates to our local pub and on coming out at eleven o'clock we stopped to chat outside the fire station doors. A car pulled up with a couple of Australian tourists in and asked the way to Chester. Now for someone who did not know the city this was a little tricky to explain, so without thinking any more about it I offered to get my car and put them on the road. I got my car and they followed me till I put them on the main road and waved them on.

On my way back a police van pulled me up and asked me what speed I thought I was doing and I replied, 'About thirty.' He asked me if I had been drinking to which I nodded. I was breathalysed, found to be over the limit and promptly taken off to the police station and charged with drink driving, not speeding or any other offence, so that was a brilliant week.

Then I had to face my wife's wrath, which believe me was fearsome. It took five months before I was called to court and the charge for driving without a current tax disc and the parking offence were dismissed. On the Wednesday I went to face the speeding charge where I found an old school friend on the bench as a magistrate. I was fined five pounds with no endorsement, and on the Friday, the big one, whilst driving over the drink limit, fined twenty-five pounds and banned for twelve months, thus ending a grim week.

On my way back from the court I decided to get away from it all, so I called into a travel agent's in the city and booked a holiday in Majorca for a week. When I got home and told my wife the result and that I had booked a holiday for the Monday she was not at all pleased. So I got another silent treatment session.

I went on duty on Saturday night so there I was sat in the back of a fire appliance as an operational fireman again. I managed to get one week's leave arranged as I was due to fly at half past seven on Monday morning. I arranged with one of the lads off another watch to come in early for me on Monday so I could get to the airport in time for the flight. On arrival at the airport I found the flight delayed by a few hours due to technical problems, but eventually we got away. What followed was the daftest week in my life, I was that fed up with everything and feeling sorry for myself that I just got on the drink for a week and this was in the days when a Bacardi and Coke was a nip of Coke and a large tipple of Bacardi. I had a very boozy week and at the end of it I realised that nothing had been gained by getting myself stewed every night so I promised that from when I got home I would not drink for the next twelve months and I didn't. I was not very proud of myself after that holiday.

Promotion

When I next went on duty another shock awaited me as I found myself called into the office and promoted to temporary leading fireman for a period of four months. This was ironic but it reminded me of what the senior officer had said before, too many qualifications; having lost my licence they were no use to the brigade or myself.

So here I was no longer one of the lads in the true sense of the word; it did not take long to find out that putting a bar on your shoulder made it a little difficult to have a good laugh and a joke with your mates when you were on duty. Some of them eyed you as one of them, an officer, and it was a situation where you could soon find yourself with a load of aggro if you were not careful, but I tried my damnedest to be fair-minded with everyone and to do the job to the best of my ability. There was a lot to be said for anyone who got promoted to be sent to another station away from the lads you had worked with for a long time.

The loss of my licence upset things a little. I was no longer able to drive my family on holiday, it was back to trains and coaches, which I found to a bit of a bind.

Being sat in the officer's seat in the front of an appliance took a bit of getting used to. I was bloody terrified half the time at the way some of the lads drove the machines, now I knew what some of the officers must have gone through with me at the wheel, but to this day I still remain a very bad passenger in a vehicle. Every week the traffic seemed to be on the increase, and driving was a very arduous and hazardous task.

As a junior officer it was one of my tasks to give the watch lectures on various subjects, but my pet theme was topography. I did not like the idea of a crew getting onto an appliance in response to the bells and finding only the driver had listened to the tannoy for the address. Consequently if he didn't happen to know where it was we could have been delayed whilst someone looked it up in the *Geographia*. So I used to turn to the crew, and in particular the newest members, and ask them where we were going. If they could not tell me I would tell them in no uncertain terms of what I thought of their attitude of leaving it to the driver to get the information. This would happen more in the very early hours of the morning.

The driver, apart from being the pump operator when we arrived at a incident, was a very important member of the crew. We were all in his hands en route to the incident, he had a lot of responsibility in getting you there as quickly and as safely as possible. Sometimes whilst proceeding to incidents you would get the idiots in cars who would not get out of the way but would deliberately try to speed away in front of you. I believe in some states in America it is a offence to not give way for a emergency appliance and I would like to see something similar over here.

The other side of the story was the number of people who would panic when they saw a fire appliance behind them. I once saw a young lady collide with a lamppost in the city centre trying to get out of the way. Fortunately she was unhurt, but as I have said before, driving a fire engine always gave me a thrill.

Usually as a junior officer at London Road you were in charge of the salvage tender or the emergency tender so you invariably went to a lot of road accidents and the like. I well remember one wild wet and windy night we turned out to seven road accidents on the trot; we had just had a long spell of dry weather and the rain had turned the roads into skating rinks.

One of these was an articulated lorry which jack-knifed on a bend and overturned, the driver being very badly trapped. The emergency ambulance from the local hospital arrived carrying a doctor and a nurse with all the specialist gear. The doctor injected the man and we got to work to free him. All the time we were working to free him he remained conscious, he told us he did this run every night and he knew it was a bad bend but it had beaten him tonight. The sad thing was although we released him he expired before we got him into the ambulance, despite all methods of resuscitation that were tried by the medical team. It turned out he was so badly crushed with serious damage to all his major organs,

We got back to the station and within minutes we responded to a car under a lorry. On arrival we saw it was a mini under the trailer of a articulated lorry. It appeared that the lady driver had ignored a crossroads in a race against the traffic lights and realising she was not going to make it had braked hard and skated under the side of the lorry. When we looked at the incident on arrival we feared the worst but on going under the trailer we found the top of the mini ripped off and the lady crouched down in the car uninjured. We removed her from the car and, although she was suffering from severe shock, she did not have a scratch on her, what a lucky lady.

Later that night we were called to take out a driver of a car who had hit a tree on the central reservation of a dual carriageway. He was dead on arrival. Just to finish off a busy tour of duty we got called to a road accident with four youths injured. They had stolen a car and skidded into a lamppost. They were all released with minor injuries but you could not help but think they could have quite easily killed some innocent pedestrian. But they were not in the least worried, their whole attitude as they were cut free from the car was that it was all a big joke. What does one do with these people, most firemen have their own ideas but they would not go down too well with the do-gooders.

One day I was asked to go in and see an ADO. He asked if I would do a day's overtime at a filming session at Granada TV, the company had hired a fire appliance and a crew to film a fire sequence in *Coronation Street*.

He asked me to ask for off-duty volunteers to form a crew and go down to the studios. This presented no trouble as everyone wanted to go, so I got five men and on the appointed day we arrived at the studios at 7 a.m. We were told to go to a caravan-type canteen and have some breakfast, this we did and we were served massive bacon sandwiches and mugs of tea.

The director then came and briefed us on what he wanted us to do. The scene was a clothing factory being burned down and we were to be shown fighting this fire. He wanted a shot of four of us in BA sets going through smoke and flames. It was all very realistic, the actual flames being piped through perforated pipes fed by bottled gas and the smoke from smoke bombs. It was all going very well until the director asked for more flames as the crew were going through a door and they turned up the gas. We got our hands very slightly singed but no one suffered any harm.

After the scene had been shot we got introduced to all the big names of the cast, one of these names was to become a favourite of all the brigade a few years later; that lady was Pat Phoenix but more of her later.

After the filming had been completed it was five o'clock and the director took us all across the road to a pub and bought us all drinks, it had been a very interesting day for us all.

Gradually I settled into my new role and was quite enjoying it but at the back of my mind was the thought that in a few weeks I would be back at square one, a down to earth fireman. However, in the short time I held the rank I learnt quite a lot about man management and delegation.

One Saturday night I went on duty to find I was detached to Moss Side for the night, so off I went. When I arrived I found an old friend was in charge, a Sub O who had a brilliant reputation as a fireman. After about an hour we got a bell to attend a fire in the footings of a precinct that was being built nearby. On arrival we found the fire to be an electric cable that supplied the tower cranes on the site. The fire was soon extinguished and whilst making my way out I slipped into a hole. As I did so I felt a terrible pain in the lower part of my back; I managed to get back to the appliance and back to the station but I was in no fit state to carry on being on duty, so one of the lads took me home in the station van.

I found I was more comfortable lying on the floor than in my bed, so this I did, and my wife called the doctor who came and diagnosed a possible slipped disc and said he would arrange for me to go to hospital on the Monday; in the meantime he left me some strong painkillers.

On the Monday an ambulance arrived and took me to hospital where after X-rays it was decided to keep me in and put me on traction, which they did but due to there being no beds empty on the ward, I was put in a private ward, with ruddy great weights attached to my feet via pulleys. I stayed like that for ten days whilst I was measured for a surgical corset. When I was discharged I was told to wear this corset at all times. This I did, whilst it was uncomfortable to wear and it certainly restricted any bending it did relieve the pain.

Eventually I felt fit enough to resume duties but I had got into the habit of wearing the corset. Whilst it certainly restricted my mobility I was able to manage, but football was out of the question, and all my lifting was done in the correct manner of bending from the knees and not the waist.

One evening on my way home a young recruit asked to speak to me. He eventually got round to asking me would it be in order to ask my daughter Carol if he could take her to the cinema. Now the manner in which he asked was great, very polite and taking nothing for granted, so I told him she was still at school and that if she agreed to go with him that was okay by me providing she was home by half past nine. He agreed to this and eventually my daughter told us he had asked her out, the result of this date was that five years later she was to marry this recruit.

Eventually the time came when I was able to get my licence back, and the first thing I did was to go out and buy a brand new car. I had saved up the money for the deposit during my ban. The big snag came when I went to insure the vehicle I got a shock at the prices quoted but I eventually got it sorted.

Chief Officer's Driver

I got my job back as a duty driver after a few weeks which was something I had not expected, but a bigger shock was in store for me. I was asked if I would like the job of the chief officer's driver, as his driver had just retired. I accepted this position and had a position in which I was my own boss, no one bothered me, all that I had to do was to be there when required by the chief. The job was a nine to five job with a few odd night trips to drive him to functions and the like. If there happened to be a serious incident the chief was going to attend I had to make myself available, so living on the station was quite convenient for me.

The week prior to the reorganisation, I was out every night driving the chief and his guests to some function or other. It seemed as if the city fathers were intent on spending money before the Greater Manchester County took over.

On Sunday, 31st March, I took the chief and his good lady wife from the town hall where they had been to another function, and I drove them to their home address where they both wished me luck. I must add that the chief appeared to be a very bitter man at not having been offered a senior position in the new set-up. The chief of Lancs County had got this position and he had made a point of putting his own officers in the top jobs. Barely any of the senior officers from the County boroughs having been given positions, the top echelon consisted of ex-Lancs

County men. This in itself caused a lot of bitterness amongst the personnel of the amalgamated brigades.

The first thing the new regime did was to announce that the bar and club room at London Road would close on the 31st March and then they built a new bar in the officers' mess at brigade HQ, talk about double standards.

When I reported back to the station with the chief's car I had no idea what my position was going to be. I went into the control room with the keys of the car and said to the senior control lady, 'These are the keys of the chief's car.' I was corrected straight away by an officer whom I had never seen before, who rebuked me, 'This is the chief officer', pointing to another officer I had never met before. As I was about to leave the control room the officer, who I learned later was to be our divisional commander, gave me an envelope to take with me.

When I got in the flat I opened it and found a letter telling me I was promoted to substantive leading fireman and was to take up an appointment at Gorton fire station; I was shell shocked.

The Shambles

Next day I transferred all my gear to my new station ready to go on duty the following night. Looking at the roster I saw that I knew most of the lads from my days at Upton Street, as this was the replacement station, so that was not too bad a start.

My first tour of duty I was introduced to my new station officer who was an old-timer from Salford fire brigade. In between turn outs we spent most of the tour wading through new brigade orders and procedures that had come into force. The obvious thing to us all was if it was one of Manchester's regulations get rid of it, it was almost childish but what else could you expect when literally overnight a brigade of three hundred and eighty men and women became over two thousand personnel.

We expected teething problems at the outset but never to the degree that we eventually experienced. To state just a few, the mobilising system that had been in use in Manchester for years was scrapped and the Lancs County system introduced. Now the County had never consisted of any city brigades, they were mostly sprawling areas with retained crews here and there, something that the city had never had. All the larger towns in Lancashire had been county boroughs, Bolton, Rochdale, Oldham and Wigan to name just a few and, for example, they decided that Manchester had sent too many appliances to a city centre shout so they reduced the number of machines attending, so in the event of getting to an incident that was well alight we had to wait for further appliances to respond to a make up call.

Another of their pigheaded schemes was that if the city station was empty of appliances they did not send in another to cover from a substation, they were soon to learn the error of their ways on that one.

The first appliances in the new brigade to have the logos removed from their appliances were of course ex-Manchester it appeared the new chief and his cohorts had a fixation on anything to do with Manchester.

One of the classic clangers they dropped which proved how vulnerable their system was, one evening the crews of a substation were sitting down to supper when they heard the sound of a two-tone horn of a fire appliance passing the station. It transpired a little later that this appliance had been directed to a incident a few hundred yards from the station and this was from a station five miles away, luckily it was only a minor incident.

If you complained or even made suggestions you were told to be quiet and get on with your job, no listening to people who had been doing the job for years. The girls in control were constantly complaining of the system of turn outs. Many years later after I had left the brigade they reverted to Manchester's mobilising system.

The rank and file of the new brigade were quite convinced that they held a weekly raffle at brigade HQ for promotion. The brigade headquarters swarmed with senior officers doing mundane jobs like operating letter opening machines, the paperwork became ridiculous so that you could no longer ask to take a bank holiday from the staff office, it had to put on paper. You were not allowed to use your common sense, they paid a man thousands a year to make a decision for you. Someone said they had a DO in charge of pencil sharpening at HQ, which would not have surprised me.

Lots of the lads were very incensed with some of the things that occurred. I remember going to a fire where the officer in charge made pumps ten. Now at large incidents if you wanted extra equipment you went to the nearest appliances and got it, but this particular time a senior officer appeared on the fireground and proceeded to go round the appliances and take the name of the officer in charge of each appliance. Days later these officers were warned that their appliances had been found not to have turned off the flashing lights and that lockers had been left open after equipment had been taken out. Now I ask anyone what were we coming to when someone has to do this, to try and justify his existence? These were the officers incidentally who never had dirty fire gear or for that matter dirty hands, was it any wonder why men, who for years had done their job so well and without prompting, were subjected to this sort of idiotic treatment, got irritated by the goings-on?

Another example was in the early hours of the morning when we were called to a building used as a joiner's workshop. It was a straightforward incident until a senior officer whom no one knew arrived on the scene and took charge and turned the incident into a BA exercise for an hour. Then when it was all over and the equipment made up he called everyone together and proceeded to hold a communications exercise with control in the early hours of the morning. It was gradually building up into a seething cauldron which had to boil over, and sure enough it happened one Sunday morning.

For years Sunday had been classed as a stand down; in other words once the equipment had been checked we were free to do our own thing. Now the new regime decided to start holding exercises in the station areas, and it came to a head one Sunday when after checking the appliances the station officer said we were going to a large hotel in the city to hold a BA exercise and that we had to go into London Road for ten o'clock. When we arrived the London Road crews met us and said they were refusing to carry out this exercise, after lots of threats and what have you from senior officers, the chief officer was informed of the mutiny. He arrived on the station and we were told to assemble in the canteen where he would address us. When he entered the mess his face was like thunder, he looked as if he was going to throw a heart attack.

He ranted on about how all he had inherited from Manchester was a load of old clapped out fire appliances and a few hundred men. At this someone at the back of the mess yelled, 'At least we are proper firemen!', and he then charged out of the mess. The idea of Sunday morning exercises died a death, the senior officers seemed to see some sense after this, but it was something I never thought I would see. All one could put this down to was the fact he could not accept that Manchester had a brilliant reputation as a fire service. Why else would brigades from all over the country or for that matter from all over the world send their recruits to be trained, the chief just had a bee in his bonnet about Manchester. He eventually went as a Home Office inspector of fire brigades, but there were lots of personnel who would not allow him to inspect their gas meter let alone a brigade. His successor was the ex-deputy of Lancs County, a man very much from the same mould as the previous chief and just as intensely disliked by the rank and file of the brigade as his predecessor. He was to soon be on the move as chief of London fire brigade, we all wished them the best of luck with him.

It was not long before we got our first Home Office inspection under the new set-up. After the usual exercise we were assembled in a circle round the inspector, after the usual pep talk the chief addressed us and said what a good modern brigade we had become, what a two-faced man.

After the chat he called one of my crew over and gave him a tongue lashing for still having a Manchester City transfer on his fire helmet. When the lad tried to explain he was shouted down, it was then that I saw the chief had a Lancs County cap badge on his soft cap so I drew his attention to this and was instantly told to get my crew together and to return to the station, again double standards.

You got to a stage where you wondered what the hell was going to happen next when you went on duty. One morning I was in the office doing the daily records when an assistant divisional officer walked in and announced that he was our new station commander, he asked the station officer what the lads were doing. He told him they were doing station routines, so he told me to get them on the yard in fire gear ready for drill. This I did, and when he came into the yard he ordered me into fire gear, and then proceeded to give us the run-around for two hours. This was with a crew that were doing about five thousand fire calls a year. You talk about getting off on the wrong foot, this fellow certainly did. After the drill he addressed us all and told us he would run the station his way and for us to forget any previous ways. It turned out he was one of the celebrated ex-junior firemen who had been recruited and during their training they were told they were the future officers.

His downfall had to come eventually and sure enough one Saturday evening we got a call to a multi-occupancy building which had a restaurant in the basement. When we arrived the basement was heavily smokelogged. Within a minute or so our new officer arrived, our station officer was around the back of the building assessing the situation. He arrived just as the fire broke through on the ground floor. He asked how many pumps should be used, this was what I had been waiting for, so I told him to decide as he was in charge and started to walk away. He called me back saying he wanted to know my opinion but I had already made my point so I suggest he use eight, which he did. When a senior officer arrived he made it ten, which was the norm, they always made a couple more than the original make up message. This fire was particularly nasty as it spread upwards through a disused lift shaft and ducting it eventually got to the fourth floor before we got it under control, it had been a nasty filthy job whilst it lasted.

We got back to the station and cleaned up the appliance and when all this was done we got ourselves cleaned up. After that I was called in to the commander's office with the station officer. He told me to sit down, then he began by saying that when he was doing his training at Moreton-in-the-Marsh they had been taught that the officer had to exercise his authority and not to let anyone undermine it. This straight away made me think we were in for a rollicking, but he went on to say that what he had been taught was not correct, as he had found out this evening, having been faced with a situation he had not been in before.

He said he had not realised the extent of the spread of fire and was not really sure of how many pumps he needed, he was grateful for my assistance and he realised how I must have felt with his attitude towards me on his first day on the station concerning the heavy drill session he had put us through. He assured me that this mistake would not be repeated. Now I admired him for this, as it must have taken a lot of guts to admit to his mistakes.

I told him there were lads on the station with twenty years' service and they would not let anyone down if they were treated right, but cross them and they could make one's life a misery. They knew all there was to know about being nice or being nasty, anyhow the outcome of that situation was that we shook hands and I left the office feeling a lot had been sorted out. I often wished that more of them could have realised their attitudes were all wrong and it got them nothing but bad feeling on the watches. The commander and I became good buddies after that, I always treated him with respect in front of other personnel but when we were on our own we used first names.

There seemed to be a different course awaiting every time you went on duty, and I was sent away to another local station to be taught a fire prevention course along with twenty more junior officers.

Then that was followed by a six-week junior officers' advancement course at Moreton-in-the-Marsh; this course had everything, how to write up reports, fight ship fires, rescues from sewers, and with every bit of theory you were ever likely to need. The facilities were magnificent, there was not a text book in existence that was not in the library, visual aids, films you name it, it was available. The messing facilities were akin to a top-class hotel, and there were three bars available plus all sorts of sporting classes. The only drawback was you were away from your family all week. We finished at 3 p.m. on a Friday and went home till Monday at 9 a.m. For anyone, but especially the younger ones on the course, it had everything to help you in advancement of your promotion prospects. I should imagine a good number of today's senior officers in brigades throughout the country have a lot to be thankful of Moreton-in-the-Marsh.

One of the junior officers whilst on this course decided he would go into Cheltenham one night, where he met a girl who turned out to be some bigwig's daughter. She invited him to a hunt ball at a hall the following week, so he hired the evening dress and went along. As he told us afterwards all the booze was free and the upper class prats ignored him when they learned of his profession, but the girl who had invited him stuck by him and asked to see him again, which he agreed to do. On his way back from the ball he was stopped and breathalysed by the police, and he was charged with drink driving. When he rang the girl a couple of days later he related the story but she told him not too worry, as her father would sort it out. He never heard any more about it. It turned out her father was rather big in the county.

A few weeks after my return from Moreton I encountered a little bit of trouble by doing what I thought was right although it was not seen that way by a senior officer. Late one afternoon we got a call to a grass fire at an allotment. Now grass fires were quite a rarity in our area. Anyhow off we went, but en route we saw a large pall of smoke ahead of us, I told the driver to slow down as approached the smoke and when we neared it I observed a two-storey building well alight on the ground floor. I directed the driver to drive up to the incident and told the crew to get two jets to work, and then I informed control that I had stopped to attend a serious fire and asked them to direct another appliance to the grass fire that we had originally been responding to.

The crew did a brilliant job of getting this fire under control, it turned out to be a store and garage on the ground floor and offices on the first floor of a wholesale fruit and vegetable merchants. As expected a senior officer arrived on the scene and after checking the situation congratulated the crew on their efforts, but a funny thing was to occur, the owner of the premises said to the officer that he had spotted the fire from his house which was across the way. He had phoned the fire brigade but before he had put the phone down the fire engine was coming round the corner, he just could not believe the speed of response and no one wanted to disillusion him. However, on going on duty next morning a senior officer came to the station to give me a reprimand for failing to attend the grass fire to which I was initially sent. Now the daft part of this was that the officer agreed with my actions but he had been detailed off by the divisional commander to give me a reprimand, and a few days later just to vindicate me a letter arrived at headquarters from the owner of the company involved in the fire, thanking the brigade for the prompt and efficient way we had handled the incident. He also enclosed a cheque for the Fire Brigade Benevolent Fund. Anyhow I never heard any more over the incident but if asked would I do the same again the answer would be yes. I would say if a life had been involved in the incident would I have been reprimanded for my actions, I believe the answer would be no, but then who knows for certain how some of those officers' minds worked.

It took about two years for the shambles they created to start to settle down to something that resembled a good functional brigade, this was the opinion of the majority of personnel with any length of service in the brigade.

At one stage in the early days of GMC, officers would rather struggle with the men they had on the fireground rather than make up the incident, one of the reasons being that if you made a incident up you were inundated with senior ranks all trying to show their authority. You sometimes had that many officers that you could have had them stamp the fire out.

The number of times I heard men wish it was time for retirement, something you never heard in the old days. The distrust between officers and men had to seen to be believed and when men started to question orders you gave, it had become unreal but the truth of the matter was the people in charge would not face the facts of how morale had sunk due to their stupid ideas. Men did not bother applying for time off because of the paperwork involved and the scant regard made to reasonable requests. If a man wanted a night off duty for some reason or other he would just ring the station and book in sick for a tour of duty, it was easier that way, and it saved them using one of their accrued bank holidays.

It would be interesting to see how much money the brigade spent in the first two years of its existence on stationery alone, ignoring the man hours spent on processing the same. Every day you had to make out a form with the facts of who was detailed off to ride which machine, in the old days this was done on a board with a chinagraph pencil and cleaned off after the dutyman had copied it into a permanent record book.

In the old City brigade we had two storemen to administer to the needs of a whole brigade. Within days of the reorganisation we had eight men to do the same job for the same number of personnel in the division.

The number of times exercises were called for at weekends only created more ill feeling and it was not long before the union seized on these stupid ideas to call a 'work to rule' policy, something that was virtually unheard of in the brigades before reorganisation. We would come on duty, check the machines and then just sit and wait to answer the bells. The lads did not like the change but it had been forced upon them until eventually the light dawned on some of the senior officers that they had to listen to the gripes the men had, and gradually they relented on exercises and FP visits during stand down periods.

So life very gradually returned to a semblance of the old times and we got back to the old routines although discipline seemed to have gone by the board. On one of the substations a man went on parade one day with his hair in a hairnet and wearing a gold earring. When the officer in charge came down to earth after seeing this apparition, he asked what the hell he thought he was playing at. His answer was that he was going out straight after duty. He was asked to remove the net and earring which he refused to do, so the officer in charge told him he would not allow him to ride a machine in the manner in which he was dressed, so after being asked again and refusing the officer in charge sent him off duty. This case was taken up by the union and the brigade backed down, consequently we had men running around with long untidy hair and multicoloured socks instead of the brigade issue. This was the beginning of a decline in standards of smartness by firemen, but I suppose it was what one would call moving with the times. However, in my humble opinion I was quite happy to carry on the way I was when I first joined the brigade.

What one must remember was when I first joined, the majority of us were ex-servicemen but when they did away with National Service the first breakdown of discipline began, but we had to carry on. The majority of the lads were great and some of them were fabulous firemen and I would have trusted my crew with my life anytime and I often did, but sometimes you got a rotten apple in the barrel.

I was told to do a probation report on one young fireman on my watch, this I did and I did not take any pleasure out of recommending that this man be dismissed as unsuitable. His performance on the fireground and his general behaviour on the station left so much to be desired, he simply did not want to learn. In my final comments I said he would become a liability and someone would get hurt trying to took out for him. The ADO of the station read the report and sent for me, he said that it appeared I was being too hard on the lad and he should be given more time to settle down, with which I disagreed, but I was overruled.

Six months or so later he was dragged out of a building seconds before the roof collapsed and this was after I had specifically told him not to enter this building under any circumstances as it was derelict and we could not see the extent of the fire in the roof timbers. When we got back to the station I sat down and wrote a report saying I would not be responsible for this fireman any more due to his total stupidity, insubordination and general lack of intelligence. He was a complete and utter liability to me and his mates, but once again I was called before the ADO and he made it clear he was not happy with the report in front of him. He accused me of overreacting, but the outcome was that I asked for a interview with the divisional commander concerning this report. He asked if I would be satisfied if he posted the man to another watch and I replied that he would be passing the buck, but never the less that is what happened. A good number of years after I retired from the job my fears were confirmed when the man brought a load of disgrace on the brigade.

Strange incidents still continued to occur, for example one Friday afternoon the bells went down for a call to a woman trapped in mud. Away we went to a house address that we were given, on arrival we were met by a paramedic who informed us that they would like assistance to remove a women from a downstairs room. We went into the house to be confronted by a horrifying sight, in the front room was a bed in which a lady of an indiscriminate age lay in a sea of filth. The room itself was waist deep in rubbish with a narrow passage to the bed. On examination we found the lady covered in solidified excrement and the like, the stench was so bad the crew put on BA sets and rubber gloves. They pulled the bedding down to put the woman on the stretcher and as the bedding came away they were confronted with open sores all over the lady, she was placed in the ambulance where she promptly expired despite the efforts of the paramedics.

The resulting investigations showed that the lady had been taken ill a good few months previously and her husband, who it turned out was mentally ill, had left her in bed, and every morning gave her some toast and a drink plus cigarettes. He told no one of the problem, and it was only when neighbours began to smell the filth in the house that someone decided all was not as it should be and sent for the police and an ambulance. No charges were ever preferred against the husband due to his mental state.

It was about this time I was asked if I was interested in a bit of part-time work, and after being told what it entailed I said I was interested. It was security work with the pop groups appearing in the King's Hall at Belle Vue.

The first one was The Osmonds, and we were lined in front of the stage to keep the audience from encroaching. Now the average age of the audience would be about fourteen years old, and the antics and offers some of these girls got up to in an effort to get us to let them into the dressing room area were no one's business, a lot of them were shameless.

Next were The Who, again the same procedure in front of the stage but this time no trouble with the audience but I did nearly get my head belted by Roger Daltrey who was swinging the microphone round.

Not being a pop fan myself I could not understand all the adulation for these overpaid groups, in fact the only one I enjoyed and who to me was a sheer professional was Elton John.

One group I witnessed were bottled up before they went on stage and the bloody awful noise and sheer ignorance was unbelievable, after the so-called show we would go round the back and see the things some of them got up to.

The money was okay for these nights and there was never any lack of lads wanting to do the job, my daughters would ask for souvenirs so I would pick up a plectrum off the stage that they had used and the girls would take it to school saying this belonged to whoever had appeared.

The residents at London Road heard on the grapevine that it was the intention of the brigade to close down all the flats at the station as the plans had been drawn up to have a new station built to replace London Road. Some of the residents contacted the local authority housing department about rehousing. Now some of the areas that were offered were unbelievable, areas of Hulme and Moss Side where the tower blocks were inhabited with every known type of scum in existence. These areas were totally unacceptable to us, someone in the housing department saw the light after they were told we worked shifts and our families would not be able to rest at night without a man in the house in these areas. They started to offer houses in the better class areas, fortunately this was not to effect me as I retired from the brigade before they shut down the station.

The time arrived when I was to receive my Long Service and Good Conduct medal, all the recipients were to parade at brigade HQ and in front of the watch committee and all the rest of the councillors, we were to be presented with the medal from the lord lieutenant of the county. This is where I upset a few people by refusing to attend, my reason being that it was just an excuse for a lot of freeloading people to attend a free booze and refreshment party at the expense of the ratepayers. My reason for not attending was frowned upon by a lot of senior officers. I did eventually receive it via the divisional commander, I was called to his office and given the box containing the medal, no handshake or thank you from him, but it is there now for one of my grandchildren.

People said to me I was being difficult, but that was not the case, if I believed something was wrong I would say so in my own way, it was the way I was brought up, to speak my mind. Perhaps sometimes I was not very diplomatic but I got my message across in my own way.

This day and age I see more bootlicking than ever before, in particular with politicians and people associated with royalty. What has happened to the upright and honest men of years gone by? People got by on their own merits, but even in the fire service that seems to have slipped away. A lot of it was not what you knew but whom you knew when it came to promotions. I saw a lot of yes men get into top jobs with this attitude. If the chief said to some of them do this or that they would fall over to do so with no regard to whether it was right or wrong, and with no regard for anyone else.

Whilst it may appear I am a bitter man as regards these things, let me assure the reader that I am not. The people concerned have to live with their conscience but then again these people were so arrogant they could not care less how they got promoted as long as they got it.

Over the next couple of years we had a number of 'work to rule' episodes, some I agreed with, others it sometimes appeared to me to be plain stupid, but life carried on, and all the time it seemed to get better for me financially, especially with my wife working full time and my doing the odd part-timer if I required anything over the norm. All the children were going well at school and my son in particular was excelling at swimming and rugby, for which he represented the county at both.

One Christmas my wife and I were discussing what to get the children for presents, one of the things was a Scalextric racing car track and cars for our son. This was bought and on the Christmas day morning I got it all assembled for him to play with but he showed no inclination to play with it. So after a few hours of my playing with it I boxed it up and put it away. After a few days he still did not appear interested in it, so when one of the lads on the station mentioned buying a Scalextric for one of his children I sold him the one I had bought. Within hours my son wanted to get the cars out and have a race. When I told him I had sold it all hell was let loose, to this day it's a standing joke between him and me that I sold his Christmas present when I got fed up of playing with it.

Getting Better

Carol's continued friendship with the recruit was blossoming but due to the fact he was from a Warrington fire station she did not see him too often. However, my telephone bill bore testimony to the fact they kept in touch a hell of a lot. Both girls were studying hard for their exams, and when they took them all the hard work paid off with both of them getting a fistful of 'A'-level passes, from which Carol went to teacher training college and Sylvia went on to university.

Our son Barrie did not have a clue what he wanted to do when he left school but he was adamant on one thing, he would never join the fire brigade. He still had another two years at school to go before his exams, and whilst he excelled in all the sporting events he took part in, his school reports always finished with: 'Barrie has the ability to do better in his academic subjects if he applies himself' but we were happy with his progress and we felt it unfair to judge him in comparison with his sisters' achievements in their studies.

Life under the new set-up settled down more each week with the older members of the brigade starting to accept the set-up; grudgingly we had to admit there were some things for the better.

An example or two of this was you no longer remained on the fireground of a large incident for hours on end, there always seemed to be fresh crews arriving at regular intervals to relieve you to go back to the station.

Under the old set-up I have seen crews turn out to a large fire at 7 p.m. and still be on the fireground at 7 a.m. the following day. Appliances were starting to be standardised throughout the brigade, the new vehicles were all Fords; one of the main complaints the drivers had of them was that they were very unstable when cornering, we believed this was due to lack of baffles in the water tanks which allowed water to slop about from side to side.

The equipment we got issued with was more up to date, but one of the big complaints was they withdrew our personal axes and just carried one or two on the appliances. Now to take away a fireman's axe was something we could not understand. I know mine had proved its worth a thousand times for various tasks which cropped up, like making a entrance to a building, breaking windows to make an entry, for chopping away debris. You could go on forever extolling the virtues of a fireman's axe, but they said it had to go, so it went.

With all the upsets that went on, fires still occurred with their usual frequency and all the problems associated with them. We found that some of the senior officers were starting to realise that working a city brigade was vastly different from the rural areas a lot of them were used to, instead of haystack fires and grass fires that a lot of them had been used to attending they were now having to cope with fires in large multi-occupancy warehouses. A example of this and, incidentally, perhaps the hottest conditions I ever encountered was one afternoon we got a call to an old converted mill which was multi-occupancy with a variety of firms occupying it. The fire was on the ground floor which was heavily smokelogged. Now a lot of these old Victorian mills had brick arch ceilings which contained the fire from spreading upwards, it also contained the heat and smoke. I was a member of two BA teams that made an entry to try and locate the fire. The smoke was really dense and conditions were nasty, but we made our way in and we knew we were not far off the seat of the fire because of the heat we were encountering.

We suddenly came up to what appeared to be a chain link fence, we tried following this down the room but it seemed to go on for ever. By this time it was time to get out for new air cylinders and a break. When we got outside I reported to the officer in charge and told him the situation, he then found a man who worked in the firm who explained that the chain link fence was there to segregate their area of the floor from another firm, the entry to this area was at the far end of the building. Asked what was in this area he replied it was a firm who made lampshades and the like.

We made another entry but this time carrying bolt croppers, we cut through the fence and eventually found the fire. We gave it a good bashing from the jet then we had to come out again as the heat was so intense, in fact I went to adjust my helmet on the way out and I could hardly bear to touch it, it was so hot. After other crews had been in and knocked the fire we went back in to see what the hell had created so much heat, we found hundreds of feet of wooden and plastic shelving loaded with what had once been fancy lamps and literally thousands of plastic lampshades, at the other end of the area was a workshop that had contained lots and lots of plastic used in the manufacture of these lampshades.

This was where the filthy smoke had come from and the fact that the heat hit the ceiling then came back down accounted for all the problems we had encountered, but as I said this had to be the hottest situation I ever found myself in, and when one thinks about it, one could understand the terrible conditions our colleagues in London found when they had the terrible tragedy on the underground at King's Cross. The conditions were very similar with heat and smoke with nowhere to go but upwards and the firemen trying to get down through this fierce heat barrier.

House fires can and do generate a lot of heat but invariably they tend to vent themselves by blowing out windows or travelling through open doors, this is one of the reasons that people are usually dead before the fire gets to them, they die through inhaling the hot gases and smoke.

I myself have seen how far people will go to in their efforts to get away from the heat and smoke, I have seen children dead in a wardrobe, under the bedding and in upstairs toilets, as I said earlier it is amazing the lengths people will go to thinking they are getting themselves into a safe position.

A story one of the old hands told me years ago about how he was on a crew that were called to house fire one evening, three children died at this house fire, but the amazing story is of how it had started in the first place. The man, who was a lorry driver, had for a number of weeks been in the habit of siphoning off a small amount of petrol from his vehicle. He had a little job on the side which consisted of making plaster of Paris plaques for a local speedway team. When they had set, he would paint these. Now one evening with two children in bed and a baby in a pram downstairs, he set about painting the plaques; he had a rag which he dipped in the petrol to wipe any smudges on the paintwork. This particular evening he soaked his rag in petrol from a can and set to work painting, noticing the rag had got rather a lot of multi-coloured paint on it so he threw it in the open coal fire, the fire flashed back to the can; he picked up the can to try and throw it out and promptly dropped it spilling the petrol on both himself and his wife, consequently they were both on fire. The wife had the presence of mind to grab the baby from the pram and then promptly passed the baby to her husband, because her clothes were also on fire and they ran out into the street. By this time the baby's clothing was on fire, and neighbours hearing the screaming had thrown blankets over the parents and baby. Someone phoned the fire brigade and an ambulance; the brigade found the fire had gone up the stairs and the two children had died, the baby also died, the parents were both badly burnt but survived – so simply started with terrible consequences.

In the middle sixties I remember being on a crew which was called to a fire in a bedroom in the middle of the morning. When we arrived a lady said she had seen smoke coming from the house across the way, so we made an entry only to be met by four men in the hallway who said there was no fire. The boss sent two men upstairs and when they came down they said there were two children apparently dead. Then all hell let loose with one of the men going berserk. The children were dead, asphyxiated by smoke from burning bedding ignited by a electric fire being in close proximity to the bed, these children had obviously panicked and gone under the bedding. Their ages were three and eighteen months. The four men had been playing cards in the back downstairs room and they had heard nothing, what a waste of young lives.

Some of the things you witnessed appeared unreal, and could have been so easily avoided, but these things happened and will continue to do so because of what human nature is all about.

When my daughter Carol was seventeen and a half she asked if Dave and herself could get engaged. Whilst my wife and I thought it to be rather a young age we agreed. I was thinking at the time that nothing would come of this as it was her first and only boyfriend and that it was just a passing phase but how wrong I was on that.

Nineteen seventy-six was to prove me wrong about our daughter's engagement, for her boyfriend came to see us and asked in the old-fashioned way for permission to get married, we agreed to the union and they set a date.

Time went by and our son eventually left school with creditable passes, he had expressed an interest in joining the Royal Navy so he went along and applied and was successful in his application but he was told there would be a waiting period. The next thing we knew he came in and said he had got a job as an apprentice motor mechanic at the Volvo agents, so off he went to work for them. With the interest in the RN waning we were happy that he had found a job for himself.

I managed to keep going in the job although it was getting more and more difficult to hide my problem, but I knew I was cheating on my mates and at the back of my mind I kept thinking about what would happen if I went down in a rescue situation and I myself had to be dragged out. But I was stubborn, the problem was not going to go away. By now I had got to the stage that going on duty was becoming an ordeal with the pain I was suffering in my back, I felt I was a liability to my colleagues. They were magic and they virtually carried me about, but I did not want to have to go out of the job on a medical disability, so I carried on the best I could with a superb team of lads looking after me.

The brigade answered a call one morning to a pub in the city centre, I was not on this call, but the lads who were related a harrowing story afterwards. On arrival at the pub they had to make an entry because there appeared to be no one about and smoke was issuing from the basement. When they got down to the basement they found five bodies under some stairs where a fire was burning, they extinguished the fire and the police were called to the incident.

It came to light after investigations that the landlord of the pub had murdered his wife and children in the early hours of the morning, and later at about 7 a.m. the cleaner arrived and he killed her. Then he went into the cellar where he placed the bodies and lit a fire, he then committed suicide by throwing himself on the fire he had started. Before having done this he emptied all the spirit stocks on the floor and opened the taps to the ale barrels allowing their contents to flow out.

At the inquest it was brought out that the landlord had received notice to quit from the brewery for some reason or other, and this had caused him to become mentally disturbed, but the lads who found the bodies had a shock. About this time I had a bit of a shock, our son told his mum and me he would like to join the fire brigade. This was right out of the blue, as he had never shown any inclination before. I tried to get him to complete his apprenticeship but no he wanted to join then.

So of his own accord he put the wheels in motion, he received his application forms and got his referees and eventually got called for his interview and medical which he passed with no trouble at all. Eventually he was told to attend the training school which at that time was still at London Road, but whilst he lived there he still had to live in at the training school accommodation about a hundred yards from his own bedroom.

He joined at a rather bad time as there were rumblings in the country as a whole about a strike in support of a pay claim, there was a lot of unrest in the brigade and the militancy which had never had cause to appear reared its head.

My injury to my back suffered another serious blow, in fact it was the finish of my career when we attended a fire at a flat. This flat had a door at the side near the stairs and another door on the front facing balcony, so to make an entry to the flat which was quite plainly on fire I decided to kick in the side door. Myself and one of the lads attempted to do this in the usual fashion; two size nine fireboots kicked together at or around the lock area, but instead of the lock giving way, we both bounced back across the balcony where I hit the balcony parapet in the small of my back. That was it, me screaming in pain lying on the balcony. The lads made an entry through the other door and there they found the reason for us bouncing back, the occupants had actually had a gas cooker plumbed in behind the door to give them more room in the kitchen. I was able to get back on the machine and get back to the station but I had to admit defeat. I was beaten with my back problem, so I made arrangements to see the doctor who took one look and immediately sent me off to hospital. By this time I was having difficulty in walking with my right leg being dragged; they took me in to hospital and again I had X-rays and tests which proved that I had three prolapsed discs and one of them was virtually smashed up. When I asked what the situation was I was told they were not prepared to operate because the chances of a successful outcome were very slight. The outcome was that I was to wear the corset at all times and the prospects of my ever being able to carry out operational duties were nil.

Here I want to jump the gun a little. Eight months after I left the brigade, whilst living in Scotland, I collapsed in the street and was taken to hospital in Edinburgh where after examination I was told that an operation would be required. I told the doctor of what I had been told in Manchester and his reply was, 'You're nae in Manchester now, laddie, you're in a proper hospital.' Three weeks later I walked down twenty-two steps out of that hospital, the proud possessor of three plastic discs and two plastic stays up the side of my spine, no pain and able to carry out a normal life.

I was sent to see the brigade doctor who informed me that having read the hospital reports he had no option but to inform the chief that I would no longer be able to carry out operational duties and that he was going to recommend my discharge on medical grounds. This was a hammer blow but in my heart I knew this was right because of the way I had struggled since the initial injury. I was put on sick leave whilst awaiting for my discharge date.

Strike

Whilst this was going on the Fire Brigade Union held a strike ballot and the members had agreed to take strike action nationally. This was the first ever national strike and it was a decision not taken lightly by thousands of men, who for years had accepted peanut rises whilst all the other jobs were getting reasonable pay settlements. So the strike took effect from the 11th November, 1977. At the outset the men thought this would only last a few days but how wrong could they be, it went on for weeks, nine in fact.

They brought in the services with their outdated clapped out Green Goddesses, and the public were given a load of gaff of how the service personnel could give them the same service as the professionals. We even had one stupid MP saying to the press that we didn't need all these firemen when the army had proved that they could do the job. What he did not say was that these lads were not allowed into buildings to fight fires, they were to stand outside and pour water into the building.

The lads on the picket lines had a great deal of sympathy for the service personnel as they had got the dirty end of the stick to cover up for a disgusting government decision not to award a reasonable pay rise. Any serviceman who rode the Green Goddesses in the Manchester area will tell you stories of how firemen turned up on firegrounds to tell them what to do, because they had been taught nothing but the basics: how to handle a jet, how to run out hose. It was painful to watch them, and in our opinion so unfair to the service personnel.

Another of the things that happened was the retained personnel throughout the country carried on their normal duties. These firemen who we classed as Trumpton men will tell you they were doing it because there was no one else; but a few of the more honest ones will tell you they were on to a good thing financially. They got so much each time they turned out plus a good hourly rate which incidentally was in excess of the professionals, plus they got a retaining fee. The longer we stayed out the more they earned but to hear the pathetic things put forward by their spokesman when asked to support the strike, they were quite happy for the brigades to stay out on strike.

With no pay coming in the strikers relied on contributions from the public, and the public donated a hell of a lot, and none more than Pat Phoenix of *Coronation Street* fame. Every day Pat passed the picket lines at London Road and on numerous occasions told her driver to stop, she would then alight and place a high denomination note in the collecting box.

Despite what a lot of propaganda-minded politicians would have the public believe, there was a tremendous amount of support for the firemen during the strike.

During the strike a lot of firemen resigned from the job because they could not pay their mortgages and other bills, and when the strike was over, the bloody-minded chief officers would not accept them back into their brigades.

My son had only been on the training school for a few weeks, and they had already been addressed by a union rep about joining the union, which they had all done, so they were also called out.

This strike generated a lot of bitterness between some officers and the men, most of the officers were members of the National Association of Fire Officers and they were not called upon to strike, but there were members of the union who decided to carry on working. These men got a rough ride when the strike eventually ended, so much so that at least two members of the brigade resigned rather than carry on trying to work with the firemen, several more transferred to other brigades, but I am sure the news of there attitude during the strike followed them to their new brigades.

I was one of many firemen who travelled down to London to lobby all the top union officials for money for the strike fund, but only one man voted to grant the Fire Brigades Union money to support the striking firemen. So much for solidarity. Strangely enough not long after the strike was called off another big union with a lot of clout put in for and got a substantial pay rise.

A story that I must tell was that a Green Goddess, which, whilst proceeding to a fire, overturned in a petrol station forecourt and some members of the crew were trapped, the crew of a passing police car told the lads on the picket line the address of the incident, and these lads went into the station, manned the emergency tender and went to the incident and released the trapped service personnel, thankfully with no fatal injuries.

A couple of weeks before Christmas 1977 I received a letter telling me I would be discharged with a pension on the 31st December. Now I had another problem, where was I going to live, seeing that I lived in brigade property. But that was solved, I soon got employment in Scotland where I had decided to go and live, and within weeks I was offered and accepted the offer of a council house.

This meant leaving my youngest daughter and my son to continue to occupy the flat at London Road till alternative housing was found for them. My daughter was preparing for her exams at her school and she wanted to stay at her school, I knew she would be looked after by my son so we agreed to her request. She finished her schooling and obtained employment as a GPO telephonist and went to live with our married daughter, so things turned out fine.

It was the done thing to have a leaving do, but due to the lads' being on strike and there not being much money about, I was not going to bother but the lads all told me to arrange a farewell. So I booked the room at the nearby railway club and organised a do. To my surprise around one hundred and fifty lads and their wives turned up; where they got money from was a mystery but I felt very honoured by their attendance.

Farewell

So ended my twenty-two and a half years in the fire service, not in the way I would have liked it to have finished.

Over the period of time I served I saw a lot of changes, not all of them for the better in my opinion, but then I accept I was one of the old-fashioned school; and now having been retired for twenty years I still follow situations in the service through my son and son-in-law.

Every year the brigade hold two reunions, one for the ex-members of the Greater Manchester Brigade and one for the City of Manchester brigade. I attend the latter and have a good chinwag with my ex-mates, most of the things I have recalled get discussed, and lots more that have faded from my memory.

To me it was a magical life and career, I will always be proud to say I was a fireman in one of the greatest fire brigades in the world and I have no doubt that thousands of firemen think the same about their own brigades.